ORLANDO
✳ FLORIDA ✳

A BRIEF HISTORY

JAMES C. CLARK

Charleston | London

THE
History
PRESS

Published by The History Press
Charleston, SC 29403
www.historypress.net

Copyright © 2013 by James Clark
All rights reserved

Front cover, top: *Courtesy of Harvey Smith of Downtown Orlando Incorporated.*
All other cover images appear courtesy of the Historical Society of Central Florida, Incorporated.

First published 2013

Manufactured in the United States

ISBN 978.1.62619.194.5

Library of Congress CIP data applied for.

To my colleagues in the University of Central Florida History Department
who have helped and encouraged me at every step.

CONTENTS

Contents

PREFACE AND ACKNOWLEDGEMENTS

For hundreds of millions of people around the world, Orlando is the home of Walt Disney World; Universal Studios Florida; Sea World; and other attractions. Nearby is the Kennedy Space Center, and east or west there are beautiful beaches.

Few know its rich history from the Indian raids of the 1800s, to the era of the cowboy and the cattle drives, to the center of the citrus industry.

In writing this book, I have been able to draw on a lengthy list of people whose research, writings and preservation of Orlando history made this book possible.

There is Dr. Jerrell Shofner, the former chair of the University of Central Florida History Department, who conducted detailed research into local history throughout Florida. It is frightening to think what historical research in Orlando would be without Sara Van Arsdel, the director of the Orange County Regional History Center. Her battle for the regional history center is legendary. Cynthia Cardona Meléndez, the center's curator, has devoted her career to saving the history of Orlando and, at the same time, provided invaluable assistance to me.

The *Orlando Sentinel* has an unusual commitment to Orlando history dating to the 1970s. The newspaper has run regular history columns written by a series of writers, including Jim Robison, Mark Andrews and Joy Dickinson, who have developed a following and produced several excellent books of Orlando history.

There are others whose work in Florida history has been vital. David Colburn of the University of Florida, Robert Cassanello of the University of Central Florida and Ben Brotemarkle of the Florida Historical Society have made significant contributions to Florida history.

Jon Findell of the University of Central Florida's Faculty Media Center was, as always, a great friend and helped make this book possible. Adam Watson of the Florida State Archives provided invaluable assistance as he has done so often in the past. Working with Chad Rhoad and Darcy Mahan at The History Press was truly enjoyable, and I am grateful for their patience.

The *Orlando Sentinel* and its various predecessors were invaluable reference sources.

I am also grateful for the help of Trish Wingerson, Frank Billingsley, Sandra Varry and Grant Heston for coming to my rescue time after time.

Without these people and resources, this book would not have been possible, and I am grateful.

Chapter 1

THE FIRST SETTLERS

For thousands of years, Florida lay beneath the sea, and as the waters receded, limestone remained. Most of the land was at or near sea level—Orlando is about one hundred feet above sea level. The first inhabitants were camels, bears, wolves and saber-toothed tigers. They fled south to avoid the approaching ice age—the first creatures to come to Florida seeking warmth. North of Orlando archaeologists found the fossils of those animals.

The first humans came to Florida more than ten thousand years ago, long after the prehistoric animals disappeared. They arrived in the Orlando area about nine thousand years ago, settling along Lake Apopka. Archaeologists discovered dugout canoes on the lake banks buried in muck. New arrivals six thousand years ago brought pottery-making skills and planted crops.

When the first European settlers arrived in the 1500s, there were nearly half a million Native Americans in the peninsula including the Apalachee, Tekesta, Calusa, Ai, Acuera and Timucuan tribes. The Timucuan and the Acuera lived closest to Orlando and sold corn to Hernando de Soto in 1539. Some of the Indians died in battles with the Spanish, but the biggest killers were diseases that the Europeans brought and spread to the Indians who had no immunity. The Indians died by the thousands. The original Indian tribes disappeared, replaced by newer arrivals, such as the Seminoles.

The first European to see Orlando was probably Pedro Menendez de Aviles, who landed in St. Augustine in 1565. A year later, he traveled up the St. Johns River and then into the Orlando area, camping at Lake Eola.

Florida remained a Spanish possession until it passed to England as a spoil of the French and Indian War in 1763. The British handed it back to the Spanish in 1783 as a result of the American Revolution. Spain went from a world power to a third-rate power and could no longer control Florida. Indians and others used Florida as a haven to strike into Georgia. Slaves from Georgia escaped into Florida, and pirates used its harbors without fear.

In 1821, facing the threat that the United States would take Florida, Spain agreed to sell it. Florida became a state in 1845, although there were many, like Senator John Randolph of Virginia, who said, "No man would immigrate into Florida...a land of swamps, of quagmires, or frogs and alligators and mosquitoes."

No one can say for sure where the name Orlando came from. There are a number of stories, and it may be that the mysterious origins of the name will never be known.

The most popular account is that the city is named for Orlando Reeves, thought to be a hero who gave his life in the wars with the Indians. The United States fought a series of wars with the Seminole Indians in the 1800s, and according to the legend, Orlando Reeves was an army soldier chasing the Seminoles in 1835. One night, the men camped at Lake Eola—originally called Sandy Beach—in what is now downtown Orlando.

Reeves was on patrol when he saw something suspicious in the lake—it looked like a log that had not been there a few minutes earlier. He realized that the "log" was an Indian penetrating the camp's defenses. As he sounded the alarm, an arrow struck and killed him. The soldiers and the Indians fought a battle, and eventually, the Indians faded back into the woods.

After the battle, the soldiers buried Reeves nearby on the banks of Lake Lawsona. He was wrapped in a blanket, and buried beneath a tall pine tree with his name carved on a tree. The carver, identified as a friend, supposedly carved "Orlando Reeves," but all that could be seen in later years was "Orlando Re—s."

With the last name impossible to read, the spot became known as "Orlando's grave," and eventually the city took the name. So strong was the belief in the legend of Orlando Reeves that, in 1939, students at Cherokee Junior High School—located between Lake Eola and Lake Lawsona—placed a stone marker near Lake Eola.

ORLANDO REEVES
In Whose Honor our City of Orlando Was Named
Killed in This Vicinity by Indians September, 1835

"How sleep the brave who sink to rest
By all their country's wishes blest."
—William Collins
THE CITY BEAUTIFUL
Erected by the students Of Cherokee Junior High School, 1939

With each retelling, the story added detail. In one story, there was one "log," in another many "logs." Reeves became a martyr and his funeral identified as the first Christian burial in what is now Orlando. There were even descriptions: he was "tall, lanky, wiry and dark complected, some of a furreigner," and "quick on the trigger."

Supposedly, the tree was cut down years later, despite the pleas of local residents to spare it.

The story is wonderful, but the problem is that it is false. There is no Orlando Reeves on any of the military rolls from the Seminole War, and there is no record of a battle fought near Lake Eola.

A second story identifies a man named Orlando Rees who owned a sugar plantation thirty miles northwest of Orlando. While traveling through the area around Lake Eola, he told friends he had carved his name on a tree, and soon stories began that it was the grave of a soldier. The myth of Orlando Reeves was born.

Naturalist John James Audubon came through in 1832, and wrote that he met Orlando Rees at Spring Garden, about forty miles from Orlando. Rees left Florida after Indians burned his home in 1835. It is entirely possible that Rees, the Indian attack, and the name carved into the tree became mixed up in the retelling and became the soldier Orlando Reeves.

Yet another version claims that a man named Orlando was leading an ox caravan to Tampa when he became ill and died near Lake Eola.

There are two versions associated with Judge James Speer, an early resident of the area. Supposedly, someone named Orlando had once worked for Speer, and the two became close. Speer suggested naming the town for his friend. In another version, Speer was a lover of Shakespeare and especially of the play *As You Like* with its leading character, Orlando.

Finding a name for the tiny settlement was not a priority for the handful of families who lived in the area. Survival from marauding Indians and carving farms out of the wilderness was foremost on their minds. There were no towns in the area, just forts to protect against the Indians.

All were in sprawling Mosquito County, created in 1824, just three years after Florida became part of the United States. The original county seat was the town of Enterprise, a port city that faded along with the era of steamboats, but at one time was the county seat of Mosquito, Orange and Volusia Counties. Compared to the surrounding area, Enterprise was practically a big city, with a population of about twenty.

In 1840, the county stretched from present-day West Palm Beach to what is now Daytona Beach, 150 miles long and 60 miles wide with just seventy-three hearty souls. The county shrank in 1828, when 1,200 of the 7,000 square miles became a Seminole Indian reservation.

Federal policy toward the Indians changed, and in 1835, Congress passed the Indian Removal Act, ordering all Indians to be moved west of the Mississippi River. The Seminoles refused to go, touching off the first of three wars. Most of the Seminoles were forced west or killed in battle, but a small band refused to leave, moving into the swamps to avoid the soldiers.

The Second Seminole War began in 1835 when the Indians launched surprise raids throughout Central Florida. That brought the army and a new policy. The army established a string of forts thirty miles apart along the St. Johns River and then west to Fort Brooke—today the site of Tampa. The government's idea was that the forts would be a day's walk apart. Soldiers on the march could travel from one fort to another and then have the safety of a fort to protect them at night.

The first was Fort Christmas in 1837, followed by Fort Maitland and Fort Gatlin in 1838. Fort Gatlin was named for Dr. Henry Gatlin, an army surgeon who died in an 1835 Indian ambush some fifty miles from Orlando. Soldiers occupied Fort Gatlin for only a few months between late 1838 and mid-1839. A decade later, during the Third Seminole War, it was once again occupied by troops.

In the Orlando area, the number of abandoned and burned-out cabins outnumbered the number of occupied cabins. When the Second Seminole War ended in 1842, the government offered land to settlers under the Armed Occupation Act. Settlers who agreed to live near the forts and become militia soldiers could have free land. Often the soldiers stationed at the forts returned as landowners.

By 1842, most of the Indians were gone, and what is now Orlando was void of people. Andrew Jernigan was one of those who accepted the government's offer of free land and arrived soon after the war ended. A settlement was named for him. He brought his family, several slaves and seven hundred head of cattle. The slaves were the first in the area. His daughter, Martha, recalled that their nearest neighbors were at Fort Reed, nearly thirty miles away. She wrote, "There were plenty of varmints in the woods, such as bears, pumas,

Christmas

A postcard from the 1950s featured one of the few buildings in Christmas. Standing in front is Santa Claus with some children. *Historical Society of Central Florida, Incorporated.*

TODAY, CHRISTMAS IS BEST KNOWN FOR ITS POST OFFICE, *sought after by people who want their Christmas cards to carry the postmark "Christmas." It began as a fort, to protect settlers and soldiers from the Seminole Indians.*

As December 1837 came to an end, work on a fort east of present-day Orlando was completed. It seemed only natural to name it Fort Christmas, since construction began on December 25.

The fort never saw hostilities, and the soldiers left after they finished the construction. The area remained unsettled for several years until the government began giving away land.

The town never had more than about 1,000 residents, but it did have a post office that was in demand during the Christmas season.

The fort disappeared, but in 1976 a replica was built on the site. And of course, the residents maintain a year-round Christmas tree.

wolves, and wildcats." The threat of Indians was always present. Martha Jernigan said that the family moved into Fort Gatlin—three miles south of Orlando—for nearly a year to escape threatening Indians. "Orlando was woods and the deer and turkeys fed all about where the city now stands." Jernigan opened a post office in his home, and the name "Jernigan" was recognized by postal officials. The mail came only twice a month.

Jernigan might be remembered as one of the great Florida pioneers, except his reputation is mixed. While he was the first permanent settler in the area, went to the state legislature when Florida became a state and served as a militia captain, he was also a murder suspect following an 1859 brawl. He escaped from jail twice and fled to Texas. His militia record was even called into question. One soldier wrote, "During the past three months, he has been either drunk or sick." He stayed away for twenty-five years, and when he returned, he was in ill health and forgotten.

Chapter 2

NEW STATE, NEW CITY

In 1845, Florida became a state, and Mosquito County was broken into several counties, including Orange County, which included Volusia, Osceola, Lake, Seminole and Brevard Counties.

In 1850, John Worthington became the first permanent resident of what would become Orlando, opening a small store in a log cabin. The census that year showed that Orange County had a population of 466, with 226 of them slaves.

Other families moved into the area. James J. Patrick bought land on Lake Conway, and James Speer bought farmland near Lake Ivanhoe in 1854. William Lovell started a steam sawmill on Lake Eola—then called Sandy Beach.

In 1854, Volusia County was carved out of Orange County, and Enterprise went with the new county. Orange County needed a new county seat. In 1856, an election was called to choose the new county seat, and the competition was fierce. Fort Reed, Apopka—then called the Lodge because it had an early Masonic lodge—and Fort Gatlin (today about three miles south of downtown Orlando) were strong candidates. Apopka was the favorite because of its proximity to navigable waters.

Judge Speer played a key role in making Orlando the winner. Only white males over twenty-one could vote, assuring that the turnout would be slight. Speer knew a militia member could vote in any district where he was on election day. Speer went to Sumter County and invited a squad of soldiers to come to Orange County for a free picnic that he scheduled for election

Conway

Immigrants from England came to Orlando beginning in the 1880s. They organized a polo team that played in an open field in what is now Dover Shores, an Orlando subdivision. *Historical Society of Central Florida, Incorporated.*

CONWAY HAS PLAYED A VARIETY OF ROLES *in the growth of Orlando. From cattle to oranges to immigrant center to a residential neighborhood, it has been home to everyone from polo players to rustlers to executives.*

Conway is just a few miles southeast of downtown Orlando, and the first settlers began coming in the 1870s. By 1874, a log cabin served as a combination church, school and meeting hall. At first, Conway was a cattle center, as rugged and violent as any to be found in the West. It is impossible to know exactly, but as many as a dozen people were killed in cattle feuds in the Conway area.

In the late 1800s, newspaper ads attracted people from England to the Conway area. They planted citrus trees, cleared land for polo fields and built a yacht club on Lake Conway.

Some of these English settlers were retired military men who came for the gentle climate. Within a few years, the polo team was challenging teams from throughout the country.

Their stay was brief; most left after the killer freeze of 1894—95. Eventually new settlers arrived, planting new trees and creating a new citrus industry. Nearly a century later, there was another freeze, and this time the citrus fields gave way to thousands of homes and schools, and the polo field became a shopping center.

day. The soldiers showed up, and Speer convinced them to vote for nearby Fort Gatlin.

Alabama businessman B.F. Caldwell owned much of what became downtown Orlando. He donated four acres for a new courthouse, and although it would be six years before construction began, it meant that the county seat would be Orlando, not Fort Gatlin. At the same time he donated the four acres, Caldwell sold his other land in downtown Orlando—about twelve square blocks today—for five dollars.

It was not much of a start, but it was enough for the post office to recognize Orlando, name John Worthington as postmaster and designate his general store as the post office. Receiving mail was no simple thing. J.P. Hughey left Orlando for Mellonville (now Sanford) and spent the first night camping outside of Mellonville. The following day, he entered Mellonville, got the mail, spent another night camping along the way and, on the third day, returned to Orlando.

County officials needed a place to meet and settled for an abandoned log cabin with a dirt floor and no windows. The sheriff, judge, tax collector, surveyor and clerk of court all set up offices in the small two-room structure. The building also housed every group in town. During the week, one room functioned as a schoolhouse, another for government offices and, on Sunday, it offered a home for the Baptists, Methodists, Episcopalians and Presbyterians.

The downtown property sold again in 1859 when the man who had purchased it for five dollars traded it for a horse and bragged that he got the better of the deal. Orlando had only a few dozen residents, and the cows roaming downtown Orlando far outnumbered the people.

The early pioneers lived in crude homes, one or two rooms made of logs. The size of the homes had no relation to the size of the family, but rather the size of the trees surrounding the home. If the trees were tall, the rooms were large; short trees meant small rooms. The roofs were wooden shingles. There were no glass windows, just openings to let in light during the day. At night, wooden shingles or pieces of cloth or leather offered some privacy and protection. Families slept on mattresses stuffed with moss or pine needles.

Chapter 3

THE CIVIL WAR

O n the eve of the Civil War, Orlando was beginning to thrive as a cattle and cotton center. Cowboys grazed their cows around lakes, while a small number of slaves cleared land and planted and cultivated cotton. Orange County cotton developed a following for its length of fiber. A three-acre plot yielded a 330-pound bale of cotton.

The 1860 census showed a population of 987, including 163 slaves, in Orange County, which included Lake, Osceola and Seminole Counties. The 163 slaves belonged to twenty-nine owners: 14 slaves were in Orlando, 99 in Apopka and Winter Garden and the rest in what is now Seminole County. The area was growing, but a significant number of the young men were about to leave.

There were some sixty thousand slaves in Florida, most of them working on plantations near the Florida-Georgia border. By 1860, Orange County had lost Volusia and Brevard Counties, where most of the slaves worked in the fields.

Orange County had only a handful of cotton plantations large enough to have a significant number of slaves, primarily near Apopka. Some cattlemen and farmers used slaves, usually one or two. There were also slaves working sugar plantations in the area.

After the election of Abraham Lincoln in November 1860, the Southern states began to talk about leaving the Union. Florida delegates gathered in Tallahassee in early 1861 to debate the matter. The Orange County delegate, William Woodruff, wanted to stay in the Union but was outvoted 62–7. On

January 10, 1861, Florida seceded from the Union and the following month joined the Confederacy. Florida was the smallest state in the Confederacy, with one critic calling it "the smallest tadpole in the cesspool of secession." But it sent the greatest percentage of its population to fight in the war.

Orlando volunteers formed Company F of the Seventh Florida Regiment, sending more than one hundred soldiers off to fight. Irvin Williams died in a Tennessee hospital; Warren Smith was wounded in Macon, Georgia; James Mitchell was shot in Atlanta; Josiah Merritt died in Kentucky; Cade Kershaw died in a Union prison; and J.R. Mizell, a member of one of the town's most prominent families, was captured at Missionary Ridge during the Battle of Gettysburg.

Only one significant battle took place in Florida, in Olustee, far from Orlando. The lack of military action in Florida meant that nearly all of the state's soldiers fought far from home, and their families were left to fend for themselves. Throughout Florida, stores quickly ran out of everything, and by 1862, shelves were empty with no hope of restocking. Blockade runners brought goods into North Florida ports, but they carried guns and ammunition for the Confederate soldiers or fancy goods destined for those in the South who still had gold and could afford them.

Twice each month, local merchant J.P. Hughey, who had earlier been responsible for mail runs, went to Gainesville with a mule team to see what supplies he could bring back for his family and neighbors. Everyone made do. Clothes were patched and re-patched, coffee and salt disappeared and nearly every Orlando family subsisted at poverty levels throughout the war. As the war dragged on, some of the slaves ran away, but most continued to work. For the cotton plantations, the problem was finding a market for the cotton.

When the war began, it appeared that it might be a financial boon to Florida. The Confederacy needed cattle to feed its hundreds of thousands of soldiers, and Florida not only had cows, but they could also be raised without the threat from the Union army. Before the war, Florida cattlemen shipped cows to the lucrative Cuban market, where the Spanish paid in gold. The Union blockade cut off the cattle trade with Cuba.

Jacob Summerlin made his fortune as the state's cattle king and was named the Confederates' state cattle supply officer. During the first two years of the war, Summerlin drove twenty-five thousand cows to the Georgia border. The cows were worth $200,000, but the Confederacy quickly ran out of gold and instead offered increasingly worthless Confederate money. Often there was no money at all, just a piece of paper acknowledging receipt of

Top: Jacob Summerlin posed for this picture in 1879 in full cracker regalia. *Florida Photographic Collection.*

Bottom: Sheriff David Mizell tried to keep the peace amid shootouts and cattle rustling. He was gunned down while trying to round up some cows. *Florida Photographic Collection.*

the cows. As the war dragged on, the cattlemen hid their cows to keep them from being taken by the Confederates.

Union troops never bothered with Orlando during the war. When the war ended in April 1865, Confederate veterans began returning home. If the war had been an ordeal, the return home was nearly as bad. By the end of the war, the Confederate army had few horses left, and many soldiers walked all the way from Virginia to Orlando—more than seven hundred miles—while others were able to catch a steamboat to ports such as Palatka and walk from there.

The end of the war meant a dramatic change in the Orlando economy, reducing cotton production. Those who continued to grow cotton found prices fluctuated wildly, and storms in 1871 destroyed much of the cotton crop. A second hurricane two years later destroyed the cotton crop again, dealing a deathblow to those who had tried to rebuild their fields after the first storm. Even those who tried to continue to grow cotton found getting it to market was difficult and soon abandoned it. As cotton fields disappeared, cattle and citrus became even more crucial to the area's economy.

Reconstruction came to the South, and the Republicans took over Florida. Abraham Lincoln favored a forgiving policy toward the South, and after his assassination, President Andrew Johnson attempted to carry it out. Reconstruction had little impact on Orlando, as the United States soldiers who enforced it were too far away. Still there were complaints from former Confederates. Thomas Fuller wrote to a friend, "When I came to Orlando shortly after the Civil War the Republicans were in control and any Democrats disagreeing with them were shot and thrown into one of the lakes…The gun was the law of the land at this time and we had to be careful." The stories about people being thrown into lakes turned out to be false, but there was violence. According to one account, when forty freed slaves attempted to vote, they "were whipped out of town by one Jack Ramey." Sheriff David Mizell "had a vicious fight on his hands" but was able to arrest Ramey.

People began moving to Orlando during the Civil War, trying to escape the horrors of war, and continued coming after the war. The family of William Holden came to Orlando and purchased 1,200 acres on what became Lake Holden. He became unpopular in the area, setting off a feud with other cattlemen.

Holden brought cattle but lost some to cattle thieves, a common occurrence in the wilderness around Orlando. He decided to fence his land, enraging other cattlemen. Fencing would remain an issue for nearly seventy years.

The cattlemen wanted their cows to be able to wander anywhere, which meant they could have more cows than their own land could support. In 1949 the state finally required cattlemen to erect fences. He found his fences cut and burned, and some of his cattle stolen. He abandoned cattle and turned to citrus, planting a large grove of over one hundred acres.

Francis Epps, the grandson of Thomas Jefferson, was one of the new arrivals. He lived in Tallahassee, where he played a key role in founding what is now Florida State University. Frustrated with the Union presence in Tallahassee, Epps moved to Orlando.

Some of those who came were freedmen who took advantage of free land to settle in Orlando. In 1866, the town had four houses, four stores, a barroom and the courthouse, along with a number of abandoned or burned-out cabins. Many of the buildings had no windows and were crude, but as a county seat, the courthouse was seeing an increase in the number of lawyers coming to town to conduct business. When they came, there was no place for them to stay. John Worthington, who had opened the first store in Orlando, built a large frame structure across from the courthouse. For a city that would one day have more than 100,000 hotel rooms, the structure was crude. It had six rooms, and in keeping with the town's other structures, there were cracks between the boards. The furniture was homemade, but the Worthington Hotel was the city's first.

Chapter 4

THE COWBOYS

The new residents found a raw frontier town. With an economy based largely on cattle, it became as violent as anything in the Wild West. Residents carried their guns, and even slept with them in case of trouble. Cattle rustling was rampant, brands were altered to hide true ownership, and fights in town were frequent. One cattleman, Bone Mizell, rode his horse into a saloon in one drunken episode.

In 1868, a band of particularly vicious rustlers was arrested, setting off widespread fear and threats of revenge. The rustlers hired the best criminal lawyers, but the case was "settled" when the courthouse was set on fire by an arsonist using turpentine and rosin. The fire destroyed the evidence, and the case was dismissed. Several weeks later, the jail was set afire. Sheriff Mizell tried to uphold justice, but as one historian has noted, "Armed cattlemen and cowboys stood around the makeshift courtroom and glared at public officials. Not one of them would testify."

In 1870, the violence reached its peak with the murder of Sheriff Mizell. Cattleman Robert Bullock said he had a bill of sale on some cattle but could not collect the money and wanted his cattle back. David Mizell and his brother, Morgan, and David's twelve-year-old son, Billy, rode out to find the cattle, located nearly seventy miles away. The three stopped to water their horses when gunmen hiding among the trees—perhaps as many as eleven—fired at Mizell, killing him. Billy said later that as his father lay dying, he urged that his death not be avenged and prayed for his killers.

Orange Avenue in 1879 was little more than a trail. This is thought to be the oldest photograph of Orlando. *Historical Society of Central Florida, Incorporated.*

Despite his pleas, a posse hunted down Mose Barber and his relatives. Mose Barber fled, and according to legend, his horse became bogged down while crossing a creek. Since then, the creek has been called Boggy Creek. Mose escaped and never returned to Florida. But his sons, Isaac and Little Mose, were killed. The feud between the Barbers and the Mizell family continued into the next century, ending when Mose's great-great-grandson married Mary Ida Mizell, a relative of David Mizell.

Jacob Summerlin moved the headquarters of his cattle empire from Bartow to Orlando in 1873, and his presence helped reduce the lawlessness.

The biggest threat to Orlando in 1870 was General Henry Sanford. Sanford's father made a fortune manufacturing brass tacks. Henry Sanford joined the diplomatic corps, serving in Russia, France and Belgium. He grew even wealthier during the war as his factory produced brass for the Union army.

After the war, he bought an orange grove in St. Augustine, then moved to Mellonville, later renamed Sanford, and bought twelve thousand acres. Sanford wanted to move the Orange County seat from Orlando to Sanford, which would have imperiled the future of Orlando. Sanford came up against

Left: Henry Sanford developed the town of Sanford and tried to move the Orange County courthouse from Orlando to Sanford. *Florida Photographic Collection.*

Below: Jacob Summerlin put up the money to build a new courthouse in Orlando to keep the county seat in Orlando. *Florida Photographic Collection.*

Jacob Summerlin, the cattle king. Summerlin had purchased two hundred acres—reportedly for twenty-five cents an acre—in downtown Orlando, including Lake Eola, and wanted the county seat to remain in Orlando.

At a meeting, the two clashed. Sanford wanted to make his town into a great city and thought making it a county seat would do that. Sanford made an eloquent speech about moving the county seat. Summerlin asked if he had finished speaking.

"I have," Sanford replied.

"Then I will make my offer," Summerlin said. "The county seat has been located here by the free will of the majority of settlers, the land has been deeded for that purpose. I stand here, ready to build a $10,000 courthouse, and if the county is ever able to pay me all right, if not that is also all right with me."

His offer was accepted, and the county seat remained in Orlando.

In 1875, Orlando incorporated and elected a mayor and six aldermen. What was strange was that there were ten elected officials, but only twenty-nine eligible voters. New boundaries expanded the city to one square mile.

Chapter 5

READ ALL ABOUT IT

THE NEWSPAPERS

The same year, Orlando got its first weekly newspaper, the *Orange County Reporter*, a weekly that struggled in a raw frontier town. It contained news and ads for patent medicines, promising cures for just about every disease. The type was set by hand, and the staff of three performed every job, from reporting the news to selling the ads. The founder, Rufus Russell, soon left, and after some more ownership changes, Mahlon Gore took over the paper.

A competitor, the *Orlando Daily Record*, deputed as a daily but failed and was taken over by the *Reporter*.

As the *Reporter* struggled, a competitor opened in 1885. An English immigrant named Latimer C. Vaughn opened the *South Florida Sentinel*, another weekly. The *Tri-Weekly Star*, was launched by some local businessmen in 1903, headed by Judge T. Picton Warlow. Both papers changed hands regularly.

Two years later, the *Star* was sold and became the *Evening Star* and converted into a daily. Meanwhile, Hudson made improvements to the *Reporter* and turned it into an evening daily. Orlando had two evening papers competing in a small town. The situation became more and more complex, and at one point, there were four papers competing for a small audience.

In 1913, the *Daily Sentinel* became Orlando's first morning newspaper, while continuing to publish the *South Florida Sentinel* for several more years. In 1914, it changed hands again and became the *Orlando Morning Sentinel*. Sunday editions were added to each of the newspapers, and an old-fashioned newspaper war began between the *Sentinel* and the *Reporter-Star*. They slashed advertising rates and conducted circulation campaigns in order to win.

In 1925, at the height of the boom, the *Orlando Morning Sentinel* and the *Reporter-Star* were sold to Texan Charles E. Marsh. The early newspaper barons focused on the major cities like New York and Chicago. Marsh purchased dozens of newspapers in small to medium-sized cities. Marsh was a crafty businessman, bankrolling oil wildcatters and even owning a streetcar line.

He sent Martin Andersen to Orlando as the publisher of his newspapers, and Andersen quickly became a force in the community. One of the things Marsh did was help his managers become millionaires. It is estimated that Marsh made nearly four dozen of his key managers multimillionaires.

He allowed his managers to buy their newspapers out of profits of the paper. In 1945, Andersen acquired both the morning and evening Orlando newspapers from Marsh. In return, Andersen gave Marsh the stock he owned in the *Macon Telegraph* and paid the balance out of profits.

Andersen, along with two or three other men, became a key player in Orlando. It was common for anyone seeking approval for a major project to see Andersen.

In 1965, Andersen sold his newspaper to the Tribune Company for $20 million. He told people that he liked the *Chicago Tribune*'s generally conservative editorial policy and thought it would continue that in the *Sentinel*. He remained publisher for a year and then retired, ending a career that began when he was fifteen years old in Greenwood, Mississippi.

Andersen named his own successor, William Conomos, who had joined the newspaper in 1953 and become editor and then general manager. In 1973, the *Orlando Morning Sentinel* and the *Orlando Evening Star* were combined into a single all-day publication. An afternoon edition of the paper was published for a few more years, and then the *Sentinel-Star* became the *Orlando Sentinel*.

The Tribune Company purchased the *Sentinel* as an investment and gave Conomos wide discretion in operating the newspaper. In 1976, the Tribune Company forced Conomos out and moved to take more control. The company's choice for publisher seemed odd. Charles T. Brumback was the paper's financial officer when he was tapped. He was quiet, conservative and seemed an unlikely choice for innovation.

Brumback turned out to be a major innovator, investing heavily in technology and becoming one of the first in the newspaper industry to see the power of computers. The newspaper was little respected within

Left: The 1940s storefront window of the *Orlando Sentinel* featured a display for Lucky Strike cigarettes, an advertiser. *Historical Society of Central Florida, Incorporated.*

Below: Around 1950, publisher Martin Andersen believed the community would support what was then a very large newspaper building on a block in downtown Orlando. *Orlando Sentinel.*

the industry when Brumback took over. He brought in a new editor, James Squires, a *Tribune* political reporter. Squires made great strides in improving the staff and making the newspaper more ethical.

Brumback became publisher of the *Chicago Tribune* and was then named president of Tribune Company. In both jobs, he strengthened the company, making Tribune an industry leader.

The next three publishers were Tribune veterans. The second, John Puerner, worked on the 2000 merger between Tribune and Times-Mirror Co., the owner of the *Los Angeles Times*. The merger turned out to be one of the worst business deals ever, saddling Tribune with $8 billion in debt. Puerner left the *Times* after five years of circulation and advertising losses and clashes with Tribune.

New management at Tribune compounded an already poor situation, and the growth of the Internet caused more problems. The Tribune Company declared bankruptcy. The *Sentinel*, which had seen its newsroom swell to more than three hundred reporters and editors, watched as scores of editors and reporters were laid off and the size of the newspaper shrank.

The newspaper has won three Pulitzer Prizes: Jane Healy for editorial writing, John Bersia for editorial writing and Jeff Brazil and Steve Berry for investigative reporting. Healy won for a series of hard-hitting editorials dealing with unbridled growth in Florida, a project originally launched by editor David Burgin. Brazil and Berry exposed a Florida sheriff who was unjustly seizing millions of dollars from motorists, and Bersia won for his editorial campaign against predatory lending practices in Florida.

Chapter 6

THE CITY TAKES SHAPE

B etween 1860 and 1890, the population of Orange County continued to grow rapidly: 2,195 in 1870, 6,618 in 1880 and 12,584 in 1890. Although the county's population grew, Orlando remained a tiny village, with less than 100 residents during the Civil War. (The population gain came despite the loss of Lake and Osceola Counties.) And land prices were increasing. Orlando was so aggressive in promoting itself that one Tampa newspaper editor wrote, "Orange County has been advertised and puffed to the four corners of the earth and has no end of land agents and speculators who manipulate the market."

In the 1870s, the town was still isolated. To get supplies, Orlando depended on what became known as the Bumby Express. Joseph Bumby obtained a mail route and decided to haul passengers and freight as well as the mail. He left Orlando early in the morning, arrived in Sanford at midday, got a new team of horses and then returned to Orlando in the afternoon.

Despite its problems, the state's Land and Immigration office reported:

Orange County—the county is now studded with orange groves, varying in extent from one to one hundred acres, and it is impossible to supply the demand for sweet seedlings of the usual age and size, for transplanting. This county bids fair to become one vast orange grove, and that without fear of overstocking the market, as the demand for Florida oranges is greater than the supply. Lake Monroe being the head of navigation for large steamers gives us rapid transportation to Savannah and Charleston.

People in Tampa complained about successful land sales in Orlando, but it did not stop Orlando businessmen from going to Tampa around 1900 looking for new residents. Certainly, the people of Tampa were well aware of the insects in Orlando. *Historical Society of Central Florida, Incorporated.*

Two men played a key role in promoting Orlando through their writings. Will Harney settled in Pine Castle and wrote about the area's charms for an Ohio newspaper, and Zelotes Mason of Apopka spread the word about that town. One pamphlet called the growth of Orlando "phenomenal as there are no oil wells, factories or mines, the population depending entirely on its orange groves, truck gardens and unrivaled climate. Orlando is built on the peel of the orange."

In 1884, Orlando got its first real hotel, the San Juan, a sprawling three-story brick building that would grow and remain open for nearly a century before being torn down to make way for an office building. At one time, the hotel overlooked the city jail, and the rooms on the jail side were always jammed on days when hangings were scheduled. At the same time, the first funeral home opened, operated by Elijah Hand. Before Hand opened his funeral home, people were buried the same day they died.

Opposite, top: Orlando's first telephone was installed in the livery stable and connected just a handful of businesses and homes. *Historical Society of Central Florida, Incorporated.*

Opposite, bottom: Pine Street in 1882. On the left is the office of one of the town's newspapers, the *Daily Record. Florida Photographic Collection.*

Pine Castle

Pine Castle's main street around World War I. The small community was eventually swallowed by Orlando. *Historical Society of Central Florida, Incorporated.*

PINE CASTLE WAS LONG AGO SWALLOWED UP BY ORLANDO, *and even though forty million people come to Pine Castle each year, they are not aware of it.*

It all started in the 1870s, when Will Wallace moved to the area and began writing columns for the Cincinnati Commercial *newspaper about the beauty of his new home. "There is nothing prettier than an orange grove in the night rain."*

Originally, the dateline on his columns read, "Orange Co. FLA," but he changed it to Pinecastle, the name of the grand home he had built on 160 acres. The names Pine Castle and Pinecastle were both used until Pine Castle became the official name.

By the early 1920s, there were about three hundred people living in Pine Castle and much talk of the future. Should Pine Castle become a city? The residents could not agree— often individual families were sharply divided—and eventually there were three towns: Belle Isle, Edgewood and Pine Castle.

The land boom went bust in 1926, slashing the town's tax revenue, and by 1929, the town government ceased to exist. Once more it was unincorporated—its status today.

Pine Castle might have vanished entirely if not for World War II. Pine Castle was home to the Florida Variety Boat Company, and during World War II, the company built storm boats used by troops crossing the Rhine River into Germany.

The small company turned out hundreds of boats in a matter of weeks. To do so, it took over surrounding roads and worked around the clock. It was the start a company that would become world famous as Correct Craft, which remained in Pine Castle until 2006, when it outgrew its plant.

As World War II began, Orlando's airport near downtown offered few ways to expand. The federal government decided to build a second field and chose land at Pine Castle, calling it the Pinecastle Army Air Field. The base was deactivated at the close of World War II and then reactivated during the Korean War.

In 1958, the name of the base became McCoy Air Force Base in honor of Michael McCoy, an air force colonel who died when his plane crashed near Orlando.

It was used again during the Vietnam war, and in 1975, the base was deactivated again and became Orlando International Airport, today one of the nation's most active airports. But when the planes land, no one ever says, "Welcome to Pine Castle."

The city also got its first telephone system in the early 1880s, although there were only five customers. P.A. Foster came to Orlando from Pennsylvania and started a livery stable, and his wife wanted to reach him when she was at home. He bought his own telephone poles and ran a line from his home to the stable, adding some stops along the way. The livery stable, the Blue Drug Store, Livingston's hotel and three individuals were able to call one another. In 1894, a true telephone system began, although the freeze sent the phone company into bankruptcy a year later. It passed through three other owners before being purchased by the Bell Telephone Company. In 1911, the first telephone directory was published, listing 498 telephones. The service cost $2.50 a month for a business and $2.00 a month for residential phones.

The first streetcar line came in 1886, a mule-drawn car on wooden rails. The city passed a law limiting the streetcar to six miles per hour. The same year, the city created the Orlando Water Works to provide water, but it collapsed in the freeze of 1894 and then was resurrected. The city had water and a streetcar, but the streets were still a mess, often muddy and always containing trash. Street care was left to the hogs that lived underneath the courthouse and ate much of what was thrown into the street. Anyone wishing to rent a horse had to give two-day's notice so that the livery stable owner could round one up. The city hired someone to gather the cows in downtown every morning and drive to an empty field near Lake Cherokee to graze for the day and then bring them back for their owners in the evening. Once

Orlando got its first streetcar in 1886. It was mule drawn and featured wooden tracks and only traveled along Orange Avenue. *Historical Society of Central Florida, Incorporated.*

Bunk Baxter is believed to be the one wrestling the crocodile. Men would bring crocodiles and alligators to town as an attraction on market day. *Historical Society of Central Florida, Incorporated.*

in a while, an alligator would stroll into town. Sometimes the alligators, or crocodiles, were brought into town on market day for entertainment. Bunk Baxter was the town's designated alligator roper and wrestler.

Despite the growth, there was plenty of open land in the heart of town—enough that in 1894 a circus pitched its tent at the corner of Church Street and Orange Avenue. But the progress did lead to one

Maitland

The train station in Maitland opened in 1880 and connected the village with the outside world and brought in new residents. *Historical Society of Central Florida, Incorporated.*

MAITLAND, LIKE TAMPA, FORT LAUDERDALE, AND SANFORD, *began as an army fort to protect soldiers from the Seminole Indians. The fort was built during the Second Seminole War in 1838 but was never used.*

It was a beautiful but isolated area offering a natural spring and seemingly unlimited pine trees. The first settlers were attracted by the offer of free land around federal forts.

By 1872, there were enough settlers for a post office to open, and the community was called Lake Maitland. Gradually, the word "lake" was dropped.

In 1873, George H. Packwood built a large building for town meetings and social events, followed by a large hotel, the Park House, which became a popular resort. Presidents Chester Arthur and Grover Cleveland stayed at the Park House.

Orange groves were planted and began producing oranges as early as 1876, but transportation was a problem. The railroad reached Maitland in 1880, opening the city to greater orange production and more settlers.

In 1885, the town was incorporated, and the first newspaper, the Maitland Courier, *began publication.*

The biggest boost came from New York businessman Louis F. Dommerich, who bought four hundred acres on Lake Minnehaha in 1890 and built his estate. He and his wife started the Maitland Library and organized the Florida Audubon Society. Dommerich was also a major donor to Rollins College.

The Dommerich home, Hiawatha Grove, a magnificent, sprawling structure, was torn down in 1954 to make way for the new homes being built to accommodate people who were turning Maitland into a suburb of Orlando.

change: the city council ordered that in the future no bodies be buried within the city limits without a special permit—the fine was fifty dollars.

Improvements to the streets came because of a law that required able-bodied men between eighteen and forty-five to spend six days a year working on the streets—although ministers were exempt, and it was permissible to provide a substitute. As the city became more civilized, fines were imposed for using offensive language, lewd conduct, public intoxication, gambling and fighting. Hours were established for saloons, and only medicine and newspapers could be sold on Sundays. Dog and cockfights were prohibited, although both continued. Orlando was a major center for cockfighting, with people—and their birds—coming from all over the country.

In an attempt to reduce fights, the city voted to stop the sale of alcohol but, four years later, agreed to allow its sale. It would be the first of a series of on-and-off votes on alcohol sales.

Chapter 7

THE RAILROAD ARRIVES

Everyone struggled with the financial problems of Reconstruction. The war had left state and local governments broke, and the lack of cash forced both to issue money on their own, known as script. The state owed a million dollars and could not pay it. A Philadelphia millionaire named Hamilton Disston offered to pay twenty-five cents an acre for four million acres. His plan to drain the land turned out to be a disaster and ended when Disston committed suicide. But it helped Orlando. As soon as he acquired the four million acres, he sold some of it to an English group, which promoted Orlando throughout England, and many of the British arrivals settled around Lake Conway.

The real growth was about to come, thanks to the railroad. Orlando remained small because it was difficult to reach, and bringing in supplies was expensive. To reach Orlando, supplies were brought up the St. Johns River, then into Lake Monroe to Sanford and then carried by cart twenty-five miles over primitive trails.

In 1880, the South Florida Railroad built a railroad from Sanford to Tampa, assuring Orlando's future, making citrus king and spelling the end for sugar cane and cotton. Former president Ulysses S. Grant, who happened to be looking for delegate support at the upcoming Republican National Convention, came to Sanford to dedicate the railroad and turn the first shovelful of dirt.

On October 1, 1880, the first train pulled into Orlando using small, wood-fired engines. It arrived to enormous fanfare, but when it was ready for the

The coming of the railroad in 1880 brought dramatic changes to Orlando. The station (near left) also caused businesses to move away from the courthouse to be closer to the station. *Florida Photographic Collection.*

return trip, the engine would not start, and the passengers and others at the station had to give it a push until the engine started.

The train left Sanford every day at 4:00 p.m. and moved on to long forgotten villages such as Belair, Bents and Soldier Creek before arriving at Longwood at 4:30, Maitland at 5:07 and Orlando at 5:40. The train returned the next morning at 7:00 a.m.

In 1881, a railroad from Sanford to Jacksonville opened, which meant that tiny Orlando was now linked to the entire nation by rail; an orange picked in Orlando on a Monday could be on a family table in New York by Thursday. The railroad boosted the city's economy but also brought a shift in downtown.

The entire town was built around the courthouse, but the businesses began to move closer to the railroad station about five blocks away. What had been Main Street lost much of its importance, and Orange Avenue became the major thoroughfare. Two other railroads, the Florida Midland Railroad and the Orange Belt Railway, brought prosperity to other parts of the county. The railroad brought so many people that three years later, the city began to build sidewalks and remove the stumps that still littered the streets. Garbage collection was even added.

The confidence spread to other areas. The school board members were so confident in the future that they decided to pay the county superintendent of schools in United States currency, rather than county script, which could only be spent at local stores. Religious denominations went on a building

Ghost Towns

In the late 1800s, Oakland seemed on the verge of becoming a major city. It had an opera house and a thriving business district. A series of fires destroyed the business district, and now it is a suburb of Orlando. *Historical Society of Central Florida, Incorporated.*

THERE ARE HUNDREDS OF THEM *all over Florida: the remains of towns that once seemed to be on the verge of becoming cities. In the far west, the dry, arid air preserves the remains of the long-forgotten towns, but in Florida, the rapid growth of underbrush and the humidity quickly reclaim the land, and it is difficult to tell that there were once people and buildings on the site. Around Orlando, there are a number of these communities that seemed to hold promise but are now forgotten.*

Vineland was going to be a major city on the southwestern outskirts of Orlando. It was originally called Orange City until the name was changed to Vineland in 1918. The promoters encouraged people to plant grapes, but a disease wiped out the crops. That is when the Munger Land Company offered five-acre parcels and threw in a 25- by 120-foot lot with each purchase. In 1912, the community had a post office. During the 1920s, there were stores, a railroad depot and 120 residents. But the Atlantic Coast Line closed the spur line, and the decline began. In 1940, the post office closed.

It turned out to be one of the most valuable ghost towns in history. Vineland bordered the land Walt Disney purchased in the 1960s, and land prices soared.

Today, Winter Park adjoins Orlando, but a century ago, the cities were separated by Wilcox and Formosa, two communities that are long forgotten. All that remains of Formosa is Lake Formosa, near the main Florida Hospital campus.

Piedmont was located between Orlando and Apopka and was founded in 1877. It was a citrus community, attracting Swedish settlers. There was a schoolhouse and a general store, and two railroads ran through the tiny town. It declined after the 1894–95 freeze but came back and by 1905 had its own post office and was growing. Lumber and citrus were shipped from the train station, but the railroad pulled out, and soon the population moved to Apopka, which had a train station. Today, residents may wonder where the Piedmont–Wekiwa Road got its name. (Wekiwa and Wekiwa are both acceptable spellings. Wekiwa is correct, but Wekiva has become the generally accepted term, even though the Seminole Indians did not have the letter "V" in their alphabet.)

There were a number of others: McDonald, Merrimack, Markham (Markham Woods Road remains), Gainsboro, Curryville and Forest City all had their moments but faded.

spree. A Union Free Church was built in 1857 and served the Baptists, Methodists, Episcopalians and Presbyterians—all on Sunday. In 1859, the Methodist Church was the first to have a minister, using a circuit rider who preached at several churches and who might be in Orlando once a month. Most of the churches used local citizens who were more service leaders than ministers. Some religions met in private homes. Now, with the city growing, the churches began to build their own structures. The Methodists bought a lot and spent $1,000 for the construction of a church—the same site where their magnificent church stands today. The Baptists built a church nearby, and other religions followed.

In 1881, Bishop John Moore purchased an entire block on Orange Avenue for a Catholic church. He built the Holy Nativity Catholic Church in 1887 and renamed it St. James the following year. A new sanctuary was built in 1952.

Cattle king Jacob Summerlin, probably the wealthiest man in the state, donated the land around Lake Eola for a city park and gave money for a school. The city got its first school building in 1870, a wooden L-shaped structure with openings for doors and windows.

Another Summerlin, Bob Summerlin, changed the name of Sandy Beach to Lake Eola under tragic circumstances. His fiancé, Eola, died from typhoid two weeks before she and Summerlin were to be married.

After the huge fire of 1884, Orlando finally purchased a fire truck. *Florida Photographic Collection.*

In the early-morning hours of January 12, 1884, a fire broke out in a wooden grocery store occupied by James Delaney. The smoke awakened his two clerks who were sleeping above the store, and they sounded the alarm. The roofs were still wet from an earlier rain, but still it spread to a nearby millinery store, then the drugstore and the offices of the *Reporter*. The newspaper offices were destroyed, including the press. Explosives prevented the fire from spreading farther. Some of the merchants had insurance, but not Mahlon Gore, the owner of the newspaper. For a time, the *Sanford Journal* printed the newspaper, and local residents helped Gore rebuild. Delaney lost his accounts in the fire, but his customers came forward voluntarily to pay what they owed.

A volunteer fire department was organized and a truck purchased, but the city could not afford horses and had to borrow some in case of fire.

Chapter 8

THE BRITISH ARE COMING

The Homestead Act passed during the Civil War lured millions of immigrants to the United States, but at first, nearly all the people moving into Orange County came from the South. That changed in the 1880s as Orlando began to advertise for people in England to come. The ads presented a glossy view of Orlando. The ads promoted land for a dollar an acre, and buyers could be gentlemen farmers while the money rolled in. The advertisements promised settlers could make at least $10,000 a year—at a time when $500 a year was a good salary.

In England, the first son of a wealthy man inherited the estate and money, while the other children received nothing. Some turned to careers in the military, and others became clergymen. Some came to Florida, aided by regular checks from home. Known as remittance men, they showed up at the post office frequently to see if their remittance check had arrived from home. Dozens responded to the advertisements and invested in land. One man thought he was buying all of Orlando, only to arrive and find that he was swindled. These settlers introduced polo to the rough-hewn area and held boat races on Lake Conway.

The British immigrants erected a building in downtown Orlando and used it for meetings and parties. Known as the Rogers Building, it is the oldest structure standing in Orlando. The freeze of the 1890s sent many of the Englishmen back home, and their club disbanded. The Rogers Building became a liquor store, then the First Spiritualist Church and then later an Arthur Murray Dance Studio. Restaurants came and went in the building, and it was falling into disrepair when a local businessman saved it.

The Rogers Building is the oldest building in Orlando. It was built by British immigrants as a clubhouse and has been home to dozens of businesses over the years. It is now owned by a businessman who uses it as an art gallery. *Historical Society of Central Florida, Incorporated.*

In addition to the Rogers Building, the British created Windermere. In 1885, the Reverend Joseph Hill Scott acquired 150 acres on Lake Butler. His son named it Windermere, after Lake Windermere in England. Beginning a century later, it became home to some of the wealthiest people in Orlando, including basketball star Shaquille O'Neal and golfer Tiger Woods. It was in Windermere that Woods's fight with his wife touched off a national storm of publicity and cost him some endorsements.

One Englishman began a lasting tradition in Orlando. Charles Lord ordered a pair of swans from England in 1910 to place in Lake Lucerne. Lord moved to Orlando in 1885 but thought often of the magnificent swans that swam on the Thames River. He bought four of them and shipped them to Orlando. The city reimbursed him for the ninety-five-dollar shipping charge. At first, the swans were placed on Lake Lucerne, but some were moved to Lake Eola because of the fights caused by one swan. More than a century later, the swans remain a fixture on Lake Eola.

Another Englishman, Leslie Pell-Clarke, built the first bicycle track in Orlando, weaving around Lake Eola and a six-hole golf course on the Lake Eola shore.

Windermere

Lake Down was the site of picnics and camping in the late 1800s. Today, it is one of Orlando's most exclusive neighborhoods. *Historical Society of Central Florida, Incorporated.*

JOHN DAWE WAS ONE OF THE BRITISH SETTLERS *who came to Orlando in the 1880s, lured by advertisements in British publications that promised a profitable life in beautiful surroundings. Dawe took a job with the Florida Midland Railroad, which ran near Lake Butler, southwest of Orlando. Dawe saw possibilities in the land nestled among three lakes. He laid out a town and named it for a lake he knew in England, Windermere. He solicited other English settlers, many of whom planted citrus trees.*

Two brothers, Joshua and Sydney Chase, arrived in 1888, purchased forty-six acres, and named their land Isleworth. They planted citrus trees, and a century later, the land became one of the most exclusive residential developments in the nation. The Chase holdings grew to include hundreds of acres, and one of the largest citrus developments in the state.

Other developers formed the Windermere Improvement Company in 1911 and began to sell lots. By 1920, there was a school, two stores, and a church. Because the area was so well planned, it largely escaped the land bust of 1926 and continued to prosper.

In 1983, the Chase Company sold all of its Isleworth property to investors led by golfing legend Arnold Palmer. He initially developed an upscale community, drawing many of his golfing friends, including Tiger Woods and basketball legend Shaquille O'Neil. Palmer's group sold the land to British billionaire Joe Lewis, who also developed Lake Nona.

Windermere has kept its small-town charm, including dirt roads and strict zoning regulations.

Chapter 9

THE AFRICAN AMERICANS

As immigrants created communities in Orlando in the 1880s, African Americans were also creating their own communities. The first African Americans in the area were slaves who escaped their plantations and found refuge with the Seminole Indians who lived in the area beginning in the early 1800s. The first slaves came to Orlando in 1843 with Andrew Jernigan. The first deed recorded shows a transfer involving thirty-seven slaves with names like Fatma, Bella, Tampa, Cyrus and Phoebus.

The African Americans created two communities in Orlando: the first near downtown known as Parramore, and the second named Burnett Town, for a former slave who came from Tallahassee in the 1880s. Burnett Town became Jonestown, named for two early settlers, Sam and Penny Jones. A white businessman built homes and sold them to African Americans. In 1884, the *Orange County Reporter* reported that the total population of Orlando was 1666, including 504 African Americans, whose professions included grocer, wagoner and laborer. Many attended the first church for African Americans, the Mt. Zion Missionary Baptist Church. The problem with Jonestown was frequent flooding, and in 1904, the floodwaters reached the tops of the small homes.

The floods might have driven the black residents out eventually, but racism played a more significant role. In 1939, the home of an African American family burned down, and the family asked for a permit to rebuild it. Jonestown became surrounded by white homes, and property owners in the area organized to stop the rebuilding. The application was denied. Two

Named for Sam and Penny Jones, Jonestown was an African American neighborhood. It was beset by floods, and white neighbors forced destruction of the homes owned by blacks. *Historical Society of Central Florida, Incorporated.*

years later, the city declared Jonestown a slum and ordered all of the houses demolished. The city gave the residents a small amount of money but not enough to rebuild elsewhere. Instead, the city moved them to Griffin Park, a public housing project in the Parramore neighborhood, thus forcing all African Americans into a single area. The city set up an area for African Americans to live between the Orange Blossom Trail and Hughey Street. In 1946, the area was jammed with African American residents, and another area near Lake Mann was added.

Once the blacks were out, the city installed flood-control measure to keep the homes of white residents dry.

The first school for African Americas was known as Orlando Black School and opened in 1886. There was no electricity, no lunch room and the school year was just five months long—if someone showed up to teach, and if there were no oranges to pick. In 1895, the name was changed to Johnson Academy.

In 1921, the school became Jones High School, named for L.C. Jones, the longtime principal who donated the land. Although it was called a "high school," at times it included first through twelfth grades. At first it was still a five-month school, scheduled around the needs of the citrus growers. It was not until 1929 that the students went to school over nine months, although the oranges still came first. In 1935, an elementary school for African Americans opened, and a junior high school came later.

Eatonville

AFRICAN AMERICANS *in the south often found it difficult to buy land from white landowners, who wanted the African Americans as laborers and worried that if blacks owned their own land, the whites would lose a badly needed labor source.*

In the mid–1880s, the community of Maitland was growing, and African Americans came to help clear the land and pick the oranges. But Josiah Eaton, the first mayor of Maitland, was willing to sell land to the twenty-seven African Americans who proposed incorporating a town. Eatonville covered 112 acres, one of the many black towns created after the Civil War. Soon, there was a newspaper, the Eatonville Speaker, *and the first school for blacks in Central Florida, the Robert Hungerford Normal and Industrial School, with academic and vocational courses that drew students from throughout the south. It continued to operate as an independent school until the public schools took it over in 1950.*

The town's two most famous citizens were writer Zora Neale Hurston and football great Deacon Jones.

Joe Clarke, the founder of Eatonville, built one of first homes built in the African American town. *Historical Society of Central Florida, Incorporated.*

The facilities at Jones High School were clearly inadequate, but the school board did nothing to improve the school. In 1951, the board voted to spend $6 million to build Edgewater and Boone high schools—two all-white schools—angering the African American community. Not a dime was to be spent improving Jones. A suit by African American leaders—with a push from civil rights leader Mary McLeod Bethune—forced the board to appropriate $1 million for a new Jones High School.

Civil rights leader Mary McLeod Bethune and Orlando attorney Paul Perkins forced the Orange County School Board to build a new Jones High School in 1951. *Florida Photographic Collection.*

The United States Supreme Court ordered schools to be integrated "with all deliberate speed" in 1954, but it was not until 1962 that Orlando's schools were integrated, and that came about only because the Orlando NAACP filed a lawsuit. John Proctor Ellis, an African American teacher at Jones High School, filed the suit when his daughter, Evelyn, was refused admission to Boone High School. School officials backed down, although it was not until 1969 that integration was complete. Durrance Elementary was the first to be integrated—the student body was made up largely of the children of air force personnel.

For African Americans in Orlando, life was brutal in the first half of the twentieth century. In 1920, African Americans attempted to vote in Ocoee, Florida, outside of Orlando. The leader of the black community was July Perry, who owned his own farm. A gang of white men broke into Perry's home, and in the battle, two of the attackers died. Perry was arrested and jailed, but a mob broke into the jail—or was let in by the sheriff—and lynched Perry on Washington Street in downtown Orlando and riddled his

Top: John Ellis was a teacher at Jones High School and president of the local NAACP when he brought suit in 1962 to force the integration of Orlando schools. His daughter, Evelyn, wanted to attend the all-white Boone High School. *Historical Society of Central Florida, Incorporated.*

Bottom: July Perry, an African American landowner in Ocoee, was killed during rioting after he attempted to vote in 1920. Some of the worst racial violence in the nation took place in Florida. *Historical Society of Central Florida, Incorporated.*

corpse with bullets. In Ocoee, there was a week of vengeance by whites who killed thirty-five African Americans and forced others to flee the town, abandoning their property. It was nearly half a century before African Americans returned to Ocoee.

Even expressing a desire for equal rights could bring violence in Orlando. In 1925, the Reverend R.H. Johnson tried to start a chapter of the National Association for the Advancement of Colored People, but he needed five members to obtain a charter. It took him four years to get the five people willing to risk harassment and even violence to fight for equal rights.

To make sure African Americans did not have any say in Orlando government, the leaders set up the aptly named White Voters Executive Committee. From 1904 to 1950, the committee in effect eliminated democratic elections. The all-white committee chose the nominees for local office, and voting in the general election became a mere formality. Even after the United States Supreme Court ruled in 1944 that African Americans could vote in the Democratic primary, Orlando continued to defy the court. Under the threat of legal action, the committee was eliminated, and blacks could vote in the primary election beginning in 1950.

The Apopka branch of the Ku Klux Klan carried out the worst violence. Membership in the Klan was widespread, including county officials and other leading citizens. In a cruel irony, the Orange County sheriff, Dave Starr, was a Klansman, and any citizen who went to Starr to complain about Klan violence could be reporting the crime to the man who caused it. John Talton, who served as chairman of the county commission three times, was a Klansman.

The purpose of the Klan was to intimidate African Americans and keep them working in the citrus fields, where they were needed to pick oranges. World War II changed the views of many African Americans who served in the military and escaped the segregation laws of the South. Now, they wanted more than a lifetime of picking oranges. The growers desperately needed laborers, and the Klan's purpose was to discourage any talk of equality.

In 1949, a white woman in Groveland—north of Orlando—claimed she had been attacked by four African Americans. Lake County sheriff Willis McCall—who denied being a Klansman but admitted to attending meetings—quickly arrested three men and launched a posse to find a fourth. The fourth man was tracked down by a posse and killed by McCall.

Orlando Klansmen organized a caravan of cars to go to Groveland. While the Orlando Klansmen were heading for Groveland, the small town's 350 African Americans were being evacuated to Orlando. Two nights later, a white mob went through the African American section of Groveland, shooting wildly and burning down three homes.

The *Orlando Morning Sentinel* made its position clear the next morning, running a front-page editorial cartoon showing three electric chairs with the captions "The Supreme Penalty" and "No Compromise." The newspaper urged the quick execution of the suspects. The violence peaked in 1951. Klansmen beat and wounded a black janitor at an Orlando elementary school after false rumors circulated that he had entered a girls' bathroom unescorted. The janitor's brother-in-law was beaten and shot to death—an apparent case of mistaken identity. An Orlando apartment complex was dynamited when the owner applied to have it rezoned for black occupants.

Late in the year, an ice cream stand in Orlando, the Creamette Frozen Custard Stand, was leveled by dynamite after the owner refused to provide separate service windows for blacks and whites at his small stand.

On Christmas night in 1951, the Orange County Klan members bombed the house of Harry T. Moore, the state NAACP leader, in nearby Mims, Florida. Moore died instantly, and his wife died a few days later.

The following month, Orange County Klansmen flogged and shot Arthur Holland in Orlando, saying it was "a lesson to other Negroes."

In February 1953, a grand jury was convened to investigate Klan violence in Orlando, and nearly one hundred witnesses were called. The jury called the Orlando Klan violence, "A catalogue of terror that seems indescribable." The grand jury indicted seven Klansmen for perjury, but a federal judge dismissed the charges because he said there was a lack of federal jurisdiction.

Chapter 10

A REAL CITY

In 1886, a directory of Florida listed Orlando as a "city" for the first time:

> *Reaching Orlando the traveler is met by energetic hack drivers, urging the visitor to stop at "The Magnolia, Charleston, and Summerlin hotels, all well-kept and reasonable in price." The city has two railroads, daily mails, express and freight offices, telephones, two newspapers, ice factory, schools, four churches owning their own buildings, and several other worshiping in halls and private homes.*
>
> *Walking down the sidewalks of Church Street, lined on both sides by substantial business houses, Orange Avenue is reached and the newcomer looks north on another prosperous business section. Truly, Orlando is a flourishing city, well worth the name PHENOMENAL."*

Nearly every home had orange trees in its yard, and there were a few small groves. But large-scale growing of oranges was impractical because there was no way to get them out of Orlando in bulk. The railroad changed that, and soon large groves seemed to be everywhere. Orlando was on its way, citrus fields were covering the landscape and the future seemed unlimited.

Then came the freeze of 1894–95. There were freezes before, but none as severe as this one. First, in the previous freezes, the citrus output had been tiny and the economic damage slight. By 1894, the entire economy of Orange County was based on citrus. The first freeze came on December 27, 1894, as the temperature fell to twenty-four degrees, killing the oranges. The

Rollins College

During the uprising in Cuba in the late 1890s, some Cuban parents sent their children to Rollins to escape the violence and attend school. *Historical Society of Central Florida, Incorporated.*

IN 1883 THE FIRST PRIVATE COLLEGE IN FLORIDA *opened in downtown Orlando, setting off a controversy that continues to today. The Methodist Church opened the South Florida Institute in 1883, although questions remain as to whether it was really a college. In 1885, the school moved to Leesburg, then to what is now Palm Harbor, Clearwater, and finally to Lakeland where it became Florida Southern College.*

The other claimant for the title for first college is in Winter Park.

In 1884, the Reverend Edward Hooker came to Winter Park to set up a Congregational Church. There was not much there, and Hooker was not impressed. The "town" consisted of one store and a handful of residents living in shanties in the swamps.

Hooker believed that the way to draw people to Winter Park was to attract a college and asked the Congregational Church to establish one. The church agreed to Hooker's request but opened the competition up to any community willing to bid.

There were five bidders: Mount Dora offered ten acres near a huge lake and seven hundred additional acres nearby that the college could sell or lease to raise money. The value was $35,564. Daytona offered $20,000 in cash and an oceanfront site. Jacksonville came up with $13,000 and a site, and Orange City came up with only $10,000.

> *Winter Park, the smallest of the five, made the biggest offer. The tiny town won with an offer of $125,000 in land and cash. It was named for Alonzo Rollins, its largest benefactor, who had made his fortune in the textile industry in Chicago. To escape the harsh Chicago winters, Rollins and his wife came to Florida, first to Palatka and then to Winter Park. They fell in love with Winter Park and bought six acres on two lakes, Osceola and Virginia, for $10,000. Then he bought an additional 120 acres for $2,500.*
>
> *When he learned of the competition for a college, he agreed to put up $50,000 and turn over his land. He continued his involvement, financing the first building on campus. He died suddenly while on a trip to Chicago but remembered the school in his will, leaving it forty acres in Winter Park. His wife survived until 1931 and left the college $222,475.*
>
> *The early students lived in temporary buildings. Even though it was new, the admission standards were tough, requiring knowledge of Latin, Greek, French, American history and a dozen other subjects.*
>
> *From its modest beginnings, both the college and the town have seen significant success.*

crop would have been able to come back, but in February, an unseasonable warm spell with temperatures in the eighties was followed quickly by a low of seventeen, killing the trees.

There was a large thermometer outside the San Juan Hotel showing guests how temperate the climate was on sunny days and to warn growers of impending freezes. On the night of the first freeze, Karl Abbott, the son of the hotel owners recalled the sense of doom

"About nine that night, a fine looking gray-haired man in a black frock coat and Stetson hat walked up the street in front of the hotel and looked the thermometer, groaned, 'Oh, my God,' and shot himself through the head. For three days the icy winds blew over a dead world. The gloom in the San Juan was something you could touch and feel."

One observer wrote, "Proud boasts about the Phenomenal City were forgotten in the rush to sell ruined groves and depart the unkind land…Orlando shrank back to its status as a sleepy agricultural town much like those in Mississippi, Alabama, Georgia and Arkansas. Instead of presidents and millionaires, hotels catered to cowboys, riding to town for a binge."

For many of the English immigrants, it was the end. One traded what had been a $40,000 grove for a ticket back to England. Proud of his record crop, Lucius Stebbins turned down an offer of $45,000 on February 6, thinking that he could get more. The next day, his crop was worthless. Alexander

The Citrus King

As part of his campaign to promote oranges and orange juice, Dr. Philip Phillips opened roadside stands. *Historical Society of Central Florida, Incorporated.*

THERE ARE A HANDFUL OF MEN *who have made Orlando what it is today, men like Walt Disney, Glenn Martin and Philip Phillips. Phillips created the modern citrus industry in Orlando and left a legacy that continues to benefit thousands of citizens decades after his death.*

His early life is murky. From the time he arrived in Orlando, he called himself Dr. P. Phillips and insisted that he be called "doctor." But his medical background is questionable. There are so many stories that it is impossible to know the truth. One newspaper reported in 1938 that he had attended New York Polyclinic, a hospital and medical school for advanced study. The problem is that the school did not grant medical degrees: it was for students doing post-graduate work. He told others that he attended Columbia University, but school officials have no record of Philip Phillips attending there.

There was also a story that he was given the title by the Red Cross for letting them use his French chateau as a field hospital during World War I, but the Red Cross has no record of naming anyone a doctor. The National Institutes of Health, which maintains detailed records on physicians, also has no record of Phillips ever being a physician. Sun Bank president Billy Dial, a longtime friend of Phillips, told one interviewer that he believed Phillips was a veterinarian.

Throughout his life, he insisted on using the title—real or not—and his name, with "Dr." attached, is on everything from a high school to the city's new performing arts center.

PRODUCE OF U.S.A.

ORANGES
GRAPEFRUIT
TANGERINES

Dr. Phillips

DR. P. PHILLIPS COOPERATIVE
ORLANDO, FLORIDA   U.S.A.   DR. PHILLIPS, FLORIDA

Dr. Philip Phillips produced 100 million oranges a year at one time, along with tangerines and grapefruits, from his Orlando headquarters. *Historical Society of Central Florida, Incorporated.*

But while his medical credentials can be questioned, his contributions to the citrus industry, to humanity and to Orlando cannot. Not only was he the largest grower in the United States, but his advances in producing and promoting oranges also made orange juice a fixture on millions of breakfast tables.

It was Phillips who developed the "flash" process, which made orange juice taste better in metal cans. He pushed orange juice as being healthy, even securing an endorsement from the American Medical Association.

He also was a pioneer in helping African Americans. Many of the black field workers found work for a few weeks a year, then had to move on to find new fields. Phillips saw to it that his employees had year-round jobs. In the era of segregation, he built a state-of-the-art hospital for blacks.

He sold his citrus property in 1954 but retained his other property. He wanted to build a model community for fifty thousand residents. He planned for shopping, offices, schools and thousands of homes with vast green space and wooded areas to retain the area's natural beauty.

Today, the area is known as Dr. Phillips, one of the finest developments in Orlando. He left his property and fortune to a foundation that each year benefits Orlando and has made nearly a quarter-billion dollars in grants since Phillips's death in 1959.

Hargrave was offered $50,000 for his home and forty-acre grove on Lake Holden, but he turned it down. The next day, it was all but worthless.

The worst timing might have been that of Cassius Boone, who owned the leading hardware store in town. He wanted to get into the citrus business and, on February 6, traded his store for an orange grove. The following day, he had nothing. Joseph Guernsey, the new owner, feeling badly about the situation, gave Boone a job in the store he had once owned.

Despite the setbacks, Orlando was making progress as a city. In 1895, the owners of a house at Delaney Avenue and Anderson Street became the first to install electricity. Two years later, John Cheney created a new water company and erected twenty-eight electric streetlights. From that, Cheney built an electric utility under a twenty-year franchise from the city. In 1923, the city purchased the electric company from Cheney for $975,000, creating the Orlando Utilities Commission.

The 1900 census showed the impact of the 1894–95 freeze: the city's population declined to 2,481, a drop of 500 from 1880. The county lost 1,000 residents over the same span.

While citrus was profitable, orange trees took years to mature. Starting over was simply not an option for many. People left so quickly that some left dirty dishes on the table. The county's population declined as nearly two thousand people moved out. The economic damage destroyed eight of the county's ten banks.

While the freeze meant ruin for many, it meant new riches for a few. Those who remained found they could buy the abandoned groves for almost nothing. The era of the vast citrus groves was a result of the freeze. The Chase family planted large groves in the Windermere area. Nick Belitz came to the area around 1913 and opened the first citrus gift business and used his profits to build a shopping center in Maitland.

Those who had the patience to wait out the post-freeze period were richly rewarded. By 1900, citrus was back. In 1910, Orange County produced more citrus than any other county, and in 1920, the county was producing one out of every four oranges grown in Florida. The buying and selling of oranges was becoming big business but was disorderly. Growers and buyers gathered in the lobby of the San Juan hotel each year to buy and sell crops. In 1903, the growers formed the Florida Citrus Exchange, putting the selling on a more businesslike basis. At the same time, the growers became more concerned with protecting their crops. A center was established for pesticide research.

In 1917, a Winter Park resident found some unusual oranges on a tree along his driveway. He called the head of the growers' exchange, W.C.

Winter Park

By 1887, Winter Park was developing into a city with stores and hotels. *Florida Photographic Collection.*

LORING CHASE CAME FOR A VACATION *but created an Orlando empire. Loring was a successful real estate salesman in Chicago who came down with bronchitis and came to Orlando, hoping warm weather would help his condition. Before he left home in the late 1800s, friends urged him to look at investment opportunities around Orlando, but he insisted he was just going for a rest.*

When he reached Orlando, a friend kept insisting he see nearby Winter Park. After repeated hounding, he agreed to take a carriage ride to see what was largely a deserted area except for some squatter cottages.

He was impressed, and with his friend, railroad owner Oliver Chapman, he purchased six hundred acres for $13,000 and began laying out a new town. He built the Seminole Hotel, and soon wealthy northerners flocked to his town.

Chase was so successful that Henry Sanford, the wealthy founder of Sanford, complained they were diverting tourists from his town.

A new train station brought in tourists. Chase took part in the effort to bring Rollins College to the town, and Winter Park became nationally known.

Temple. It turned into the Temple orange, which would revolutionize citrus sales. It had a sweeter taste and a bright-orange rind. From that single tree, a staple of the citrus industry grew.

In Winter Garden, Hoyle Pounds developed the rubber tractor tire, which made working in the sandy groves easier.

Some who lost crops in the freeze found new ways to make money. John B. Steinmetz came to Orlando from Pennsylvania and planted a grove, built a packinghouse and waited for the money to start rolling in. The freeze destroyed those plans, but Steinmetz adjusted and turned the packinghouse into a skating rink, installed a slide at the springs and built a dance pavilion, creating Orlando's first attraction, drawing local visitors and tourists from around the country. George Russell was doing well with his pineapple crop until imported pineapples undercut him and forced him out of business. Russell also joined the resort business, building a pavilion on Lake Ivanhoe known as Joyland.

Others turned to lumbering and built sawmills and turpentine stills. Those lumber mills became important as the citrus industry made its resurgence, producing orange crates and pallets for the citrus growers.

Chapter 11

A REFINED CITY

As they had during the Civil War, Orlando's young men signed up to go marching off at the start of the Spanish-American War. Nearly one hundred members of the Orlando Guard were sent to Tampa. The war lasted just 123 days, and there were far more volunteers than necessary. The Orlando soldiers missed the boats to Cuba and were sent to Huntsville, Alabama, where they sat out the war.

The city became less of a frontier town with cowboys wrestling alligators in the streets and men riding horses into saloons. Now, these men opened businesses and built fine homes. In many ways, the train brought civilization to Orlando. The city even began to pave its streets. The first street was paved with clay brought from Bartow and linked the Rogers Building (the British Club) on Pine Street with the train station.

Still, the civilization was not quite complete. One local businessman owned two saloons and a livery stable on Church Street, and the neighbors were complaining. The complaints became so great that in 1907, the city held an election and, by two votes, outlawed alcohol sales. On election night, the two saloons and the livery stable went up in flames. The fire department responded, but the driver of the fire truck lost control of the horses, and they sped past the fire. He later claimed the lines to the horses were incorrectly hooked up, and the truck sped by the fire.

The rise of civilization brought the city its first opera house. Although it was called an opera house, it was home for all of the city's entertainment. One opera singer, the well-known Emma Thursby, was visiting a brother in Melbourne and agreed to give a performance to raise money for a new Episcopal church. The opera house was used for traveling shows, and minstrels appeared frequently. There were religious services on Sundays, and big city events were held there. It was a money loser for the owners and became a skating rink, a center for wrestling matches and later a movie theater. But once theaters were built especially for movies, the opera house was torn down and became an auto dealership.

In 1884, Braxton Beacham Sr. moved to Orlando and made his fortune growing celery. In 1907, he was elected mayor and leased the Phillips Theatre. He built his own theater in 1921, the Beacham. At first, it was a vaudeville theater with acts traveling a circuit from other smaller towns. In 1936, Beacham switched to first-run movies, becoming the premier movie house in Orlando. The Beacham held a strange secret. The vaudeville performers usually stayed across the street at the Angebilt Hotel. Often, the fans mobbed the stars. To help the stars avoid the crowds, a small tunnel was built under Orange Avenue between the theater and the hotel.

The city's nickname had been "The Phenomenal City," but around 1900, what was known as the City Beautiful movement swept the nation. The original plan came in response to the overcrowded tenement districts in large cities such as New York, Cleveland, Chicago, Philadelphia and Wilmington. Orlando held a contest in 1908 for a new nickname. The entries included "The Magic City," "The Queen City" and "The Picturesque City," but the winning entry was "The City Beautiful." For Orlando, it meant planting hundreds of oak trees.

In 1892, Mrs. Phillard, a widow, invested her money in building seven four-room cottages with the idea of renting them and having a stable income. But their location, about a mile from downtown, was too far out in the country at the time. She offered to trade the cottages for a residence she could live in for the rest of her life.

Several women organized what they called "a cottage hospital association" as the city's first hospital. The women built a two-story building on Phillard's site and began accepting patients. Downstairs was a ward for men and upstairs a ward for women. A bed cost twelve dollars a week. Private rooms cost twenty-five dollars a week. The Episcopal Church acquired it in 1895, and it served the community for twenty years, until it ran out of money. Two local doctors, John McEwan and D.C. Christ, saw the need for a real hospital and turned to the community for contributions. In 1918, Orlando

In 1909, the Florida Sanitarium told prospective patients, "If you are sick, come and get well." The sanitarium became Florida Hospital. *Florida Photographic Collection.*

The Florida Sanitarium and Hospital changed its name to Florida Hospital in 1970. This early building, shown here around 1940, was replaced by soaring towers. *Florida Photographic Collection.*

Orange General Hospital opened in 1918 south of downtown. The original building was torn down and replaced by a major health care complex called Orlando Health. *Collection of the author.*

General Hospital opened, and despite numerous name changes, it continues to serve the city as Orlando Health.

The Seventh-Day Adventists came to Orlando in the 1880s and took over a tubercular sanitarium in the small community of Formosa—which was annexed into Orlando in 1925. They established Florida Sanitarium and Hospital with two doctors and four patients. The Adventists already had a hospital in Battle Creek, Michigan, that combined modern medicine with good food, sunshine and relaxation. The Florida Sanitarium—known locally as "the San"—was successful, and a new building was built in 1912. By 1918, the hospital had forty beds.

In 1913, Seminole County split off to form its own county with Sanford as the county seat. In seventy years, what had started as a single county with seven thousand square miles became a county with one thousand square miles.

The influx of people created a new economic model for Florida, one based on tourists. Initially, the tourists flocked to the coastal areas. Henry Flagler built his railroad stretching from Jacksonville to Key West, while Henry Plant developed the west coast.

The automobile came to Orlando in 1905 and within a few years car parades became usual occurrences. This one was held on Orange Avenue. Notice that in most of the cars the steering wheel is on the right-hand side. *Historical Society of Central Florida, Incorporated.*

The advent of the automobile meant people could travel, but there were not many roads. The first automobile came to Orlando in 1903, owned by Dr. J.J. Harris. It was steam powered, "which at times seemed badly affected. It wheezed and gasped, coughed and sputtered; sometimes its temperature rose and it plunged deliriously into a tree or fencepost." It created such excitement that when the women of St. Luke's Guild wanted to raise money, they arranged to have Harris offer rides for ten cents. The car carried just one passenger at a time, and there was a long line to travel a few blocks in downtown.

The first gasoline-powered car came in 1905, an Oldsmobile owned by P. Batchelor. The speed limit was set at five miles an hour, and the city announced a one-dollar fine for blowing the horn.

A Landmark Building

The Grand Bohemian Hotel replaced the old Dodge dealership building, which had passed through a number of owners over the years. *Kessler Collection.*

IT IS A TINY PIECE OF LAND, *just two-thirds of an acre, but it has a rich history. Located at the corner of South Street and Orange Avenue, it was the site of a home beginning in the 1880s and then a tearoom opened in 1920. Three years later, the building was moved, and construction began on a six-story building.*

It was different because the primary tenant was the I.W. Phillips Dodge Agency, and instead of sprawling as most car dealerships do today, the dealership had cars on the first floor and the service department on the second floor. It meant the structure had to support the cars, and it was the first building in Orlando using stone and reinforced concrete. The

The Dodge dealership on Orange Avenue was unusual because it was a vertical dealership with the showroom on the first floor and the service area on the second floor. *Kessler Collection.*

concrete beams were poured in place, and the concrete floors were extra thick. The upper four floors were offices.

The Dodge dealership moved out within a few years, and the building became all offices. A tenant, American Fire & Casualty Company, took over the building in 1928 and remained there until 1975. The building was sold several times until a company announced plans to gut the building. But the extra-thick concrete floors made it difficult to work with the building, and in 1996, it was demolished and turned into a parking lot.

Then Richard Kessler came along. Kessler was a top official of the Days Inn chain before striking off on his own. In an age when downtown hotels were closing and being torn down, Kessler saw a need for an upscale hotel in downtown Orlando. He approached two architects, who told him he could never build what he wanted. He was not going to be deterred, and a third architect showed him how it could be done. The result was a 250-room hotel—the Grand Bohemian—that quickly became a landmark and gathering place. From that beginning, Kessler expanded his hotel empire with more upscale hotels in downtown locations.

Chapter 12

THE TOURISTS

In 1916, the federal government began a program to build highways. The main road for tourists was the Dixie Highway, stretching from Canada to Miami which opened in 1925. The Dixie Highway was a network of roads with one coming down the middle of Florida through Orlando, and a second road went down the east coast. Cheney Highway was built to connect Orlando to the highway running along the east coast. The roads connected Orlando to the Midwest and a third of the people in the nation. It meant someone could leave the snows of Chicago and drive to sunny Orlando in two or three days.

The railroad brought the first boom in 1880, and the boom of the 1920s was powered by the automobile. The people who came in cars were called "tin can tourists." The joke was that they arrived with twenty dollars and one shirt and never changed either.

By 1925, the city had two tourist camps, the sprawling San Juan Hotel added eight stories and the new Angebilt Hotel soared to eleven stories. Contractor Joseph Ange moved to Orlando in 1913 to build the Yowell-Duckworth Building. He named his new hotel after himself but sold out two months later. The hotel was the finest in town, home to the University Club, two radio stations and elite dining facilities. Other hotels were built, including the Orange Court, the Wyoming and the Avalon. The magnificent Alabama Hotel was constructed in Winter Park.

Dr. William Wells watched the construction of the Angebilt hotel and knew there was no quality hotel for African Americans. The Jim Crow laws of the time kept hotels in the South segregated, and African American travelers had

The San Juan started in the 1800s and, by the 1920s, sprawled along Orange Avenue. It advertised that every room had its own private bath. *Florida Photographic Collection.*

Opposite, top: A postcard promoting Orlando from around 1920. *Collection of the author.*

Opposite, bottom: The Wigwam Village motel on the Orange Blossom trail was certainly the city's most unusual. It was a favorite in the 1940s and 1950s, but as the Orange Blossom Trail declined, so did the motel. It was torn down in 1973. *Florida Photographic Collection.*

Orlando's Star

Buddy Ebsen learned to dance at his father's studio in downtown Orlando. The lessons took him to New York and stardom. *Historical Society of Central Florida, Incorporated.*

BUDDY EBSEN CALLED HIMSELF *a "five-million-to-one long shot." He became a major Hollywood star in a career spanning more than half a century, but he still recalled swimming in Orlando's lakes in the 1920s.*

The son of immigrants, the family moved from Illinois to Florida to find a warmer climate for Ebsen's mother. They settled in Palm Beach, where the family struggled to make a living. While playing baseball there, a ball struck his Adam's apple, and the injury caused his trademark gravelly voice.

The family moved to Orlando around 1920 and built a small house downtown, where his father gave dancing lessons. His father doubled as a physical education teacher in the local schools. Ebsen took ballet lessons but quit to concentrate on sports. He excelled at Orlando High School, where the school yearbook said, "Ludolf, better known as Buddy, won the reputation of being one of the best guards OHS has ever had. He was strong on both offense and defense. He had the old grit and fight that it takes to make a football player."

To help the family financially, he worked as a soda jerk at the Angebilt Hotel coffee shop. In his spare time, he played with friends. "We'd go swimming, that was the cheapest recreation that we could do. Good swimming at Lake Virginia, Lake Gatlin, or Shirttaill Lake where you went in nude. It's now the heart of a posh subdivision."

Gradually he returned to dance, not as a ballet dancer, but doing some of the routines that were the rage in the 1920s. "One day I went to a matinee at the Bijou Theater, and they had vaudeville acts, and I saw an act called the Dixie Four and they did soft-shoe dancing. It's the first time I had ever seen tap dancing, and I got so excited that I ran all the way home from the theater and said to my father, 'I saw the kind of dancing that I want to do.'"

He tried out his dance routines at a small theater on the corner of Orange Avenue and Pine Street. Although he enjoyed dancing, he stuck with his plan to become a doctor. He spent a year at the University of Florida, but the family's precarious financial situation forced him to drop out after one year. The Depression had come to Florida, and the Ebsen family was hit very hard. "My father gave dancing lessons for a dozen eggs," he said.

He enrolled at nearby Rollins College, where he played on the football team and for the first time thought about becoming an actor. He took a drama course and then headed for New York with $26.25 in his pocket—a loan from his sister. He worked as a soda jerk waiting for his break, which came on Broadway, then movies and finally television as Jed Clampett on the Beverly Hillbillies *and as the ace detective on* Barnaby Jones.

difficulty finding hotels, restaurants and even restrooms open to them. Wells built a small hotel that entertained the African American elite of the era: Ray Charles, Ella Fitzgerald, Count Basie and Duke Ellington. The coming of integration in the 1960s meant the end of the Wellsbilt. African Americans could stay in finer hotels, and the Wellsbilt became a flophouse and closed in 1970. It was acquired by the City of Orlando and turned into a museum.

The automobile and the booming economy set off a land rush in Florida. Land that sold for a few dollars an acre in 1915 was worth thousands of dollars a decade later.

An event in 1911 that appeared to be a disaster for Orlando turned into one of the best things to happen to the city. A fire swept through much of the business section, destroying the train station and many of the orange packinghouses along the tracks in downtown. The destroyed structures were made of wood, and the city ordered all wooden buildings replaced with bricks and steel, touching off a building boom and modernizing the city.

Two large department stores drew shoppers to downtown. The Dickson-Ives store was remodeled and a brick front added. Across the street, the three-story Yowell-Duckworth building went up. In 1911, the Pastime Theatre became the first movie theater in town, and the opera house later became the Lucerne Theatre. The large Phillips Theatre opened in 1916, and the landmark Beacham Theater came four years later. In 1915, a bus line started, connecting Orlando, Ocoee, Winter Garden, Winter Park and Maitland. People began buying cars, and the traffic became so heavy that the Confederate memorial statue, which stood in the middle of the intersection at what is now Magnolia Avenue and Central Avenue, had to be moved to Lake Eola.

Taft

IN 1911, PRESIDENT WILLIAM HOWARD TAFT *passed through Orange County on the presidential train. The plan was to stop for a few minutes and give Taft an opportunity to wave to the crowd. Someone forgot to stop the train, and Taft chugged through Orlando without stopping.*

Still, the citizens wanted to honor Taft's nonappearance and decided to name a small community a few miles south of Orlando for him. It was the final name for a small community that had gone through a number of names since people began moving in when the railroad arrived in 1882. It was originally called Newelton after the first resident, who failed to make money and sold his land. In 1900, Michael Smith moved in, opened a turpentine camp and named the community Smithville.

Ownership changed again in 1909, along with the name—it became Prosper Colony. The new owners placed advertisements in the Saturday Evening Post *encouraging people throughout the nation to buy land.*

The ads failed to mention one significant fact: the area frequently flooded, and in 1910, a serious flood destroyed crops and forced the settlers to flee.

Growth was slow after that. A train station was built, along with a Baptist church, a school and a post office, and a new brick road linked the community with the outside world.

The 1920s brought the land boom to Taft, but the hurricane of 1926 destroyed homes, and the collapse of land prices led to defaults by settlers. World War II brought new prosperity and growth in the form of the Pinecastle Army Airfield (later Orlando International Airport), and the small community began to carve out a role as a major supply district for the airport and Orlando with sprawling warehouses and rail lines.

Taft remains unincorporated, with only 2,200 residents, and has been swallowed by the city of Orlando.

Opposite, top: Customers crowded into the Yowell-Drew store in downtown Orlando when it reopened after being remodeled in 1926. *Historical Society of Central Florida, Incorporated.*

Opposite, bottom: The Beacham Theater on Orange Avenue featured both live acts and movies and even had a secret tunnel to the Angebilt Hotel. *Historical Society of Central Florida, Incorporated.*

Despite prohibition in the 1920s, liquor was widely available in Orlando. Raids were regular events. Dave Starr, a Klansman who later became sheriff, is on the right in the bowtie. *Historical Society of Central Florida, Incorporated.*

Originally the city used pine straw to cover the dirt roads, keeping down the dust and covering the mud. But the straw did not last long and the city began making its roads out of clay, but that was in short supply. The city turned to bricks for the city streets—many are still there a century later. By 1916, there was a brick road running from Sanford to Kissimmee.

World War I came to the United States in 1917, and again Orlando's boys went off to war. The Orlando soldiers fought primarily in the Second Florida Regiment. They were sent to Alabama for basic training, and some fought in France. The war was a boon for the area's farmers, who saw crop prices soar with the demand for food in England and France. When the war ended, Orlando celebrated with a rally on Armistice Day.

Spring Training

SPRING TRAINING FOR BASEBALL TEAMS *became popular in the 1890s, and by the early 1900s, it was firmly established. The early sites included Hot Springs, Arkansas, Tulsa, Oklahoma, New Orleans and even Honolulu. In 1889, the Philadelphia Phillies came to Jacksonville, becoming the first team to train in Florida. In 1913, the Chicago Cubs and the Cleveland Indians came to Florida, and by World War I, there was a Grapefruit League in Florida. Professional baseball came to Orlando 1914, and a stadium that became Tinker Field was built in 1923, seating 1,500.*

The Cincinnati Reds were the first major league team to have spring training in Orlando, arriving in 1923 and remaining for a decade before leaving for Tampa. The Brooklyn Dodgers trained at Tinker in 1934 and 1935, then the Washington Senators—later the Minnesota Twins—moved in. After spring training ended, the Senators' AA team played at Tinker. Except for three years during World War II, the Senators/Twins remained in Orlando until 1990, when they moved to Fort Myers.

Baseball great Joe Tinker and his wife, Mary, retired to Orlando when his baseball career ended. He became a successful real estate salesman, using his fame to draw buyers. *Historical Society of Central Florida, Incorporated.*

Minor league baseball first came to Orlando when the Orlando Caps of the Florida State League played in 1919–20, followed by the Tigers, Bulldogs, Colts, Gulls, Seratomas, Flyers, Dodgers, Twins and Juice.

The last team to play at Tinker was the Orlando Rays, a minor league affiliate of the Tampa Bay Rays that played in Orlando for several years before moving to Montgomery, Alabama.

The stadium is named for Joe Tinker, a baseball great who played a role in the growth of Orlando. Tinker played for the Chicago Cubs and the Cincinnati Red Stockings and became famous for the double-play combination of Tinker-to-Evers-to-Chance—so famous that a newspaper reporter wrote a poem about them.

After his playing career ended, he moved to Orlando and went into the real estate business, building an office building in downtown Orlando and houses throughout the area. He was successful until the Florida land boom went bust in 1926. Tinker had to abandon his real estate business and return to baseball. He retired to Orlando, where he died in 1948.

Today, Tinker Field is at risk. It is in poor repair, and although it is on the National Register of Historic Places, it may be moved to a new location.

The Orlando Board of Trade issued a brochure promoting the city:

> *Orlando and Orange County are expanding and developing at a 137.7 percent pace, which proves that "the City Beautiful" is destined to have a population in 1930 of from 25,000 to 30,000 people...Thirty-three miles of brick streets and about 35 miles of sidewalks...Seventy miles of brick highways in Orange County...The Florida Sanitarium* [now Florida Hospital] *located two miles north of Orlando at Formosa Station is a medical institution giving the same system of treatments as the famous Battle Creek Sanitarium...There are 150 real estate dealers in Orlando...The summers in Orlando are preferable to those "endured" by some in the northern states. The summer nights are delightfully cool...Heat prostrations are unknown.*

The postwar period saw two national events that had far-reaching implications. Women got the right to vote in national elections beginning in 1920. Prohibition also started after World War I. It had a profound impact on the coastal areas of the state, with miles and miles of inlets that were perfect for smuggling illegal liquor from Cuba and Bimini. There were plenty of dramatic raids, but it was not difficult to find a drink. Some thought there was actually more drinking in Orlando during Prohibition than before. That became obvious in 1929 when the Chief of Police L.G. Pope was indicted for bribery, embezzlement and illegal possession of liquor. The community obviously was not too concerned with the charges—Pope was acquitted. He remained on the job and the following year launched a war on men wearing sandwich boards who were everywhere on the city streets pushing land and houses.

When Prohibition ended 1933, beer returned to Orlando. In 1935, the sale of package liquor was approved, and Rausch Inn became the first licensed club, but there were still plenty of unlicensed clubs, and police closed down the Flamingo Club and the dives on Church Street.

Chapter 13

THE BOOM

The airplane was growing in popularity and practicality. In 1919, a cow
pasture was turned into an airfield, and the Orlando Aerial Company
began offering rides. The next year, new owners bought the airplane and
launched a flying school. In 1922, Orlando Airlines began offering service
to most Florida cities, but only for one passenger at a time. In 1927, the
city purchased land about four miles from downtown bordering Lake
Underhill. The original purpose was to help supply the growing city with a
steady water supply. As the popularity of flight increased, officials realized
the land would be perfect for an airport. In 1928, nearly forty thousand
people turned out for the opening of the Municipal Airport. Pan American
Airways announced that Orlando would be included on flights to Cuba and
Puerto Rico.

By the 1920s, the Florida land boom was well underway. It was not
uncommon for land to change hands a few times in a single day, always at
ever escalating prices. New construction was everywhere, and not a week
went by that a new housing development was not announced. Although the
greatest growth was along the coast, the Orlando area saw its share. In Winter
Park, developers announced plans for thirty housing developments, but only
a handful were built. The population more than doubled in the 1920s, from
19,890 to 49,737 in 1930. In 1925—the height of boom—Orlando issued a
record number of building permits, and soon the city had one hundred miles
of brick paved streets. Office buildings and hotels replaced the ramshackle
wooden buildings that had made up downtown.

Ed Nilson came to Orlando in 1922 and started Orlando Airlines. His two-seater plane flew passengers, took aerial photography and offered flying lessons. *Historical Society of Central Florida, Incorporated.*

This view of Orange Avenue looking south in the 1920s is unusual for two reasons. First, it ends at Lake Lucerne. A causeway named for former Major J. Rolfe Davis was built later. Also, the tranquil setting would be replaced by offices, hotels and city hall. *Historical Society of Central Florida, Incorporated.*

Flying High

Pilot Bessie Coleman was living in Orlando when she was killed during an exhibition in Jacksonville. *Historical Society of Central Florida, Incorporated.*

BESSIE COLEMAN BECAME FAMOUS—*the first American woman to earn an international pilot's license—and was making Orlando her home when she died in a fiery crash in Jacksonville.*

Coleman was born in the village of Atlanta, Texas, in 1892 to a dirt-poor family—one of nine children whose parents made sure they received an education. When she was twenty-three, she headed for Chicago, where her brothers lived. After working as a manicurist and a restaurant manager, she decided to learn to fly. With the help of Robert Abbott, the founder of the Chicago Defender, *she went to Paris to take flying lessons. As the first licensed black pilot and first American female pilot, she became a celebrity and a prominent speaker.*

A speaking tour brought her to Orlando in 1926, when she met Reverend Hezakiah Hill and his wife, Viola, and stayed with them in their home. She made plans to open a beauty shop in Orlando to provide a steady income between air shows. The tour was to raise money to buy an airplane—her first had crashed—and she met Edwin Beeman. The Beeman family had an interest in aviation for a very unusual reason. The family founded a chewing gum empire based on gum using pepsin. Pilots liked it because chewing gum equalized ear pressure, and the antacid in pepsin helped calm their stomachs during rough flights. Beeman had purchased a home in Orlando and met Coleman. He helped pay off the final installment of her new plane.

With her new plane, she headed to Jacksonville for an exhibition in her Curtiss JN-4, or "Jenny." While rehearsing, the plane crashed, and she died. The first funeral ceremony in Jacksonville drew more than five thousand people. Then her body came to Orlando, and Reverend Hill held a second ceremony at his Mount Zion Missionary Baptist Church. The church was packed, and the next morning, more than five hundred turned out at the train station to see her body off to Chicago, singing "My Country, 'Tis of Thee."

Miss America

IN 1926, THE EKDAHL FAMILY MOVED TO ORLANDO *after emigrating from Sweden. Their daughter, Margaret, found work at a lunch counter at the Yowell-Drew Department Store in downtown Orlando.*

She moved to Tampa with her parents and was crowned Miss Tampa and then Miss Florida in 1928. Ordinarily, she would have headed to Atlantic City to compete in the Miss America contest, but the contest was facing financial problems and that year suspended operations—it would not resume until 1933. Instead, the winners went to Miami Beach for the poorly organized Miami National Beauty Contest, which everyone still called the Miss America contest.

Orlando's first beauty queen died tragically after a brief stay in the spotlight. *Florida Photographic Collection.*

Margaret finished third in the competition and went home. But Orlando businessman R.B. Brossier, a friend of the Ekdahl family, was not about to let it end there. Brossier had been active in the newspaper business and had contacts everywhere.

Brossier charged that the official winner, Alberta McKellop, was not really from Calfornia. It turned out that to fill out the contest, organizers had simply assigned women to states. Six of the "state" winners came from Shamokin, Pennsylvania. Miss California had traveled from Oklahoma. There were other problems: the contest organizers had run up thousands of dollars in hotel and food bills and were being sued. The Seaboard Coastline Railroad was suing for unpaid train tickets.

That still left Margaret behind Miss Texas, Janet Eastment. Once again Brossier came to the rescue. He found that Eastment had been married—an automatic disqualification.

The contest officials elevated Margaret to the top spot, but Miss Texas refused to surrender the crown, silver loving cup and $2,500 in cash she received. She said she was divorced and was technically a "Miss."

Ekdahl went on a nationwide tour but did not like the travel. After an appearance in Connecticut, she announced her engagement to band leader Will Osborne, which may have been a publicity stunt and nothing more was ever heard of the engagement.

She went to Brazil in 1930 to take part in the Miss Universe competition, but she and others were left stranded when a revolution broke out.

Tiring of travel, she wrote to a friend, "I prefer the quiet home life with mother, father and the children." She took a job as a clerk at Dickson & Ives.

On June 20, 1932, just months after she returned home, the twenty-year-old was rushed to the hospital, where she died the next day of peritonitis.

It would be another seven decades before Orlando got a genuine Miss America with no controversy. Ericka Dunlap attended high school in Orlando and graduated from the University of Central Florida. She won a number of local beauty contests before becoming Miss Florida in 2003—the first African American to be a Miss Florida—and the following year she was selected Miss America.

Orlando's best-known beauty queen is certainly Delta Burke. In 1974 at the age of seventeen, the Orlando native became the youngest Miss Florida in history. She went on to become a television star.

The city grew physically, annexing suburban areas. Exclusive-sounding neighborhoods such as Country Club Estates, Princeton Court and Spring Lake Terrace sprung up. But dozens of other "developments" were merely a promoter's dream. Signs popped up on empty stretches of land announcing that a new development was coming. "Will we have water? Yes! Will we have electric lights? Yes!" Often the developers went as far as building an entrance, usually a grand arch. A few laid out roads, but most never got any further.

College Park was one of the successful developments. The builders concentrated on smaller homes for less affluent people and found a winning formula. The founders named the streets after colleges—Princeton, Harvard, Yale—although the community did not have a college of its own. In one ad, the developers announced that lots were available for $1,500 to $4,000.

T.G. Lee acquired two cows and a calf and started a dairy business, grazing his cows near downtown Orlando. Elsewhere along Main Street—now Magnolia Avenue—the boom led to more construction. Both the State Bank of Orlando and Trust Company and the Orlando Bank and Trust built ten-story buildings, Dickson-Ives built a new four-story department store, and across the street, Yowell-Drew added a fifth floor and a three-story annex. The city also got its first chain store, an A&P grocery store on Church Street.

In 1924, the *Saturday Evening Post*, the largest circulation magazine in the country, featured an article about Orlando:

> *Orlando is a flourishing city of 17,000 population, a city of beautiful homes and wonderful outlook, where it is built around twenty-two freshwater lakes—so many evidently that it has always been able to see itself perfectly mirrored and thus avoid the ills of so many cities; such ills as graft, and filth, and jim-crack building, and eagerness to snatch for individual enrichments the things that belong to all men.*
>
> *The Orlando people are passionately addicted to whisking strangers around the city and explaining all about it—all about the lakes and the four new bank buildings that were built during 1923, and the two new 10-story buildings; and how all four of the 10-story buildings in town were built entirely by local capital, without a cent of outside help; and how land in the business section of Orlando is worth $2,600 a front foot; and how the city is crowded with visitors, in spite of the two new hotels; and how nobody knows how the visitors are going to be taken care of; and how Orlando will have a population of 30,000 by 1930.*

The economic decline began in 1925, and by the end of the year, half-finished structures had been abandoned and the "binder boys" were already heading north, often by freight train. In early 1925, *Forbes* magazine warned investors to avoid the Florida land boom.

The boom caused massive problems for the Florida East Coast Railway, which had a single line and was swamped by the demand for building materials heading south and crops heading north. (The railroad's solution was to borrow money to add a second track, which led it into bankruptcy.) The two other railroads, the Seaboard Air Line Railway and the Atlantic Coast Line Railroad, also reported gridlock. Those who wanted to build were told about the delays, and many left discouraged.

In early 1926, a giant ship sank in the mouth of the Miami harbor, blocking access to the harbor and further delaying entry of supplies. Then a massive hurricane struck Miami. It was later described by the United States Weather Bureau as "probably the most destructive hurricane ever to strike the United States." It was so vicious that no one is sure how many people were killed. The death toll estimates range from 325 to 800. The winds reached 150

The emphasis was on "dread," in the name of the golf course that opened in 1924 in College Park. Named Dubsdread, it was built during the land boom to serve the growing number of golfers who came to Orlando. *Historical Society of Central Florida, Incorporated.*

miles an hour. Hurricanes had no names then, and this was simply known as The Big Blow.

As if the storm was not severe enough, the publicity in northern newspapers was even worse. The *New York Times* claimed that thousands had died and said that there were "scores of towns razed or flooded." Another newspaper claimed "Southeastern Florida Wiped Out." Any hope of a comeback was destroyed by another hurricane in 1928 and the Wall Street crash of 1929.

A development was planned for Loch Haven Park—now the home of the Orlando Museum of Art—but was canceled when it became clear there would be no buyers. Bankruptcies soared.

For a time, construction projects kept going strong, even after the bubble began to burst. When it did burst, one of Orlando's biggest developers, Carl Dann, said, "It finally became nothing more than a gambling machine, each man buying on a shoestring, betting dollars a bigger fool would come along and buy his option." While it lasted, it had been

Bithlo

IN THE EARLY 1920S, *anything seemed possible in Florida. A barren patch of land could become a great city; a swamp might be transformed into an exclusive resort. Perhaps Bithlo could become a thriving city?*

The city started out grandly. In 1912, Henry Flagler's wife named the town after the Seminole word that meant either "outlook" or "canoe"—no one was ever sure. It was a stop along Flagler's East Coast Railway Okeechobee Branch.

The railroad drew the interest of the lumber companies, and by 1914, Bithlo was on its way. There were large forests of pine and cypress trees, and by 1920, three lumber companies were busy chopping and shipping. A school opened at the end of World War I, and in 1920, an ambitious plan was laid out for a city. There were to be five miles of roads and hundreds of homes. By 1922, seven homes were built, and the town was incorporated. The opening of a major highway seemed to guarantee Bithlo's future.

To show its faith in the future, the city issued $80,000 in bonds for electric lights, a water plant and more paved roads. The investors thought the additional money would propel the city forward. But the land boom was turning into the land bust, and by the time the collapse came in 1926, only seven more buildings had been constructed.

The decline was slow but steady. The forests were stripped, and the lumber companies left. The town was too isolated, and the school closed in 1929. The town council stopped holding meetings in 1941, and the trains stopped coming in 1944.

The town defaulted on its bonds and after World War II became a site for dumping waste.

exciting. Developments held celebrations to mark their openings, and large crowds turned out. The developers hired brass bands, offered free airplane rides and gave away door prizes to lure buyers. Some Orlando residents put signs in their windows reading "NOT FOR SALE" to discourage people from dropping by and making an offer. In Orlando, the Atlantic Coast Line Railroad built a large new train station starting in 1926. It opened in early 1927 when six thousand people turned out for the dedication. The railroad had spared no expense, expecting the massive influx of tourists and new residents to continue to grow. The architect was sent to California to look at Spanish-style buildings for inspiration. But even as the band played, and railroad executives made bold predictions about the future, the bust had begun.

Land prices had escalated wildly beginning at the end of World War I. It was not uncommon for prices to double and triple in a single day. There were so-called binder boys who showed land to prospective buyers

The Tire Man

THE FLORIDA LAND BOOM OF THE 1920S *was great for Hoyle Pounds. But the more successful Pounds became, the greater the damage to Orlando-area roads, and the more unhappy motorists became.*

Hoyle Pounds opened a garage in Ocoee in 1914 and, a few years later, moved to Winter Garden to open a Ford dealership. In 1918, he sold nine tractors to the citrus growers in the area. As the land boom gained momentum, so did his tractor sales. In 1926, the year the boom peaked, he sold forty tractors.

The problem was that the tractors had metal tires with cleats. The cleats grabbed the soil, but on the highways, they tore up the roads. The boom had led to a massive road-building program, and soon people were complaining about the condition of the roads. Laws were passed banning tractors from highways, reducing their value to orange growers with more than one grove.

Pounds was an engineering major at the University of Florida, and he began trying to find a solution to the problem. He believed he had found it in the large rubber tires used on oil-drilling equipment. The tires were hard rubber and could support the weight of the tractor. The size of the rubber tires caused a new set of problems, as they turned faster than the metal wheels and had traction problems. He fixed those problems and received a patent for his airless tires.

His invention changed life on the farm. The tractors no longer damaged highways, and they provided greater mobility not only for tractors but also for all farm equipment.

Pounds remained in Winter Garden, and over the years he received national recognition for his contribution to agriculture. He later became the largest Case Tractor dealer east of the Mississippi River, and he even played a role in helping develop the Snappin' Turtle lawn mower with a friend from Georgia. Pounds became the nation's first Snappin' Turtle dealer.

He died in 1981, but his business carried on.

and accepted a down payment, or binder. The new "owners," did not want to own the property but figured they could sell it at a profit before any additional money was due. The property might change hands dozens of times in a matter of days. It was a giant game of musical chairs and could continue as long as there were enough people to keep buying. As one person said, "We ran out of suckers to sell to and started selling to each other."

Zora's Home

IN HER LIFETIME, *Zora Neale Hurston experienced some of the grandest highs and heartbreaking lows one person can have. She once wrote, "Mama exhorted her children at every opportunity to 'jump at de sun.' We might not land on the sun, but at least we would get off the ground.' Hurston jumped at the sun but, in the end, returned to earth.*

She was born in Alabama but moved to the small village of Eatonville, outside Orlando, when she was an infant. She always claimed she was born in Eatonville, writing, "I've got a map of Florida on my tongue."

She dropped out of school and went to work, ending up as a domestic in a white household. The woman she worked for arranged for her to finish high school and exposed her to books.

Zora Neale Hurston wrote about her experiences growing up in Eatonville. She shot to fame in the 1930s, but died broke and forgotten. *Florida Photographic Collection.*

She was on her way, attending Howard University, Barnard College and Columbia University. Her first novel, **Jonah's Gourd Vine**, *received glowing reviews and established her as part of the Harlem Renaissance, a movement featuring leading African American writers and artists.*

She followed with **Mules and Men**, *which one critic called "the greatest book of African-American folklore ever written." Her novel* **Their Eyes Were Watching God** *is a young black woman's coming of age in rural Florida.*

She returned to Florida and faded into obscurity. She was falsely linked to two young boys, and her reputation was destroyed. "All that I have believed in has failed me," she wrote.

She took a job as a maid in a south Florida home, but when the family found out that their maid was famous, she was fired. Alone and broke, she died in Fort Pierce in 1960.

The Atlantic Coast Line built its new terminal south of downtown in 1926. The railway was expecting traffic to increase, unaware that a major economic downturn was coming. *Collection of the author.*

The Orlando Commercial Bank and the State Bank both failed. The local chamber of commerce tried to encourage people with a full-page advertisement in the newspapers stating that the city "is unafraid...undaunted by disaster." Brave words, but the economy would continue to decline. The magnificent Angebilt Hotel declared bankruptcy.

Chapter 14

THE DEPRESSION

The land boom mirrored the growth of the citrus industry in Orlando. Following the freeze of 1894–95, citrus became big business. Large groves were everywhere, controlled by a small number of individuals and families. By 1926, there were a dozen packinghouses processing and shipping thousands of crates of oranges to destinations throughout the country. The leading citrus grower was Dr. Philip Phillips, who always claimed to be a physician. He owned groves from Orlando to Tampa, growing oranges and grapefruit. He also did research into citrus, coming up with new methods of processing and selling fruit, and was a master salesman.

The Dr. P. Phillips packing operation was producing 100 million oranges a year—the most in the world—and he was building the world's largest citrus packinghouse just outside the Orlando city limits, opened in 1928.

While it seemed as though Orlando had the citrus industry to fall back on if land prices collapsed, the citrus business had its own problem. In 1929, the Mediterranean fruit fly was discovered in orange trees in the Hamlin Grove at the intersection of Mills Avenue and Marks Street near downtown. The county was quarantined, and fruit shipments were banned. Fruit already picked and oranges still on the trees were ordered destroyed. Every grove had to be inspected. In Orlando, national guardsmen set up roadblocks to inspect vehicles to make sure the flies were not being taken outside the area. Total production was cut by more than half. The ban was lifted after six months, but half a million boxes of fruit were destroyed.

Dr. P. Phillips built the largest orange processing plant in the country on his property southwest of Orlando. *Historical Society of Central Florida, Incorporated.*

The fruit flies caused Phillips to rethink his citrus business. Not only was the Mediterranean fruit fly causing problems, but oranges themselves also had a limited shelf life. The solution was to turn it into orange juice to extend the shelf life and make it a more practical crop.

Producing orange juice had its own problems. When canned, orange juice had a metallic taste, and consumers rejected it. He opened a plant near downtown Orlando to develop a better-tasting juice. Starting in 1929, his researchers spent two years trying hundreds of ideas before coming up with what was called the "flash" pasteurization process that improved the taste. He gave away free samples of his new juice, and sales soared. The fruit fly was eradicated, and the citrus industry climbed back to prosperity.

The collapse of land prices—in 1930, it was possible to buy land for as little as a quarter an acre—along with the fruit fly, devastated Orlando. When the rest of the nation joined Florida's depression in 1929, tourists from the north drastically curtailed their visits. By 1933, just two banks remained. When newly inaugurated President Franklin Roosevelt declared the bank holiday

Radio and Television

RADIO STATIONS CAME TO THE NATION *beginning with KDKA in Pittsburgh in 1920. Few people could see commercial possibilities for the new medium, and radio stations were often started by churches, colleges, newspapers and department stores, which used the stations for promotion or experimentation.*

In 1924, Rollins College professor E.F. Weinberg convinced the school to open its own radio station. The new station was WDBO—Way Down By Orlando—and housed in a small wooden building on campus. The new station broadcast for just sixty-five minutes a night and had just one employee who did everything for $250 a year.

Professor Weinberg asked the school to give him $600 to operate the station in 1925. The school thought the figure was too high and gave the station away. The station moved to downtown Orlando under the ownership of the Orlando Broadcasting Company. The programming ranged from farm reports to piano recitals to popular music.

In 1954, the radio station added a television station, the first in Orlando. It was primarily a CBS affiliate, but as the only station in town, it also broadcast programs from NBC, ABC and the Dumont network. It went on the air on June 3, 1954, but only showed a test pattern for the first month before beginning programming. Even when it expanded its programming in 1956, the hour between 9:00 a.m. and 10:00 a.m. was reserved for showing the test pattern so that viewers could adjust their television sets.

Both the radio station and the television station were sold in 1957 to the Cherry Broadcasting Company of Rhode Island. It changed hands a number of times, at ever escalating prices, until the Washington Post purchased it and the call letters changed to WKMG—in honor of Washington Post publisher Katherine M. Graham.

WMFJ was the second television station in Central Florida, although it was licensed to Daytona Beach. Wright Esche bought it and changed the call letters to WESH—after his name. It broadcast from Volusia County but built a studio near Winter Park in 1960. It was not until 1991 that WESH moved its entire operation to Orlando. Like WDBO, WESH passed through a series of owners and is now owned by Hearst Television.

WLOF-TV went on the air in 1958 as an ABC affiliate. The original call letters were those of a local radio station. In 1963, the call letters became WFTV. It passed through several owners and is now owned by Cox Broadcasting.

Orlando's Channel 35 has had the most improbable history. It began broadcasting as a UHF station in 1974 without a network affiliation. The station featured lots of reruns, children's programming and sports. Like many UHF stations, WSWB struggled. In the days before cable television became a major force, UHF stations were often difficult to find on a dial that was separate from the dial for channels 2–13. In 1975, the financial problems became overwhelming, and the station declared bankruptcy.

The bankruptcy of WSWB had far-reaching consequences. One of the bidders was Ted Turner, then a little known Atlanta television station owner. The legal maneuvering was complex, and Turner did not get the station and instead used the money to found his Cable News Network. The Meredith Corporation ended up with control of the station, and eventually Fox purchased it.

WMFE began in the late 1950s as WISE, a locally owned instructional television station with programming aimed at kindergarten and elementary students in seven Central Florida school districts. In 1970, it became a public television station. It was sold to the University of Central Florida in 2012.

shortly after taking office, the federal government looked at the books of both banks and refused to allow the First National Bank & Trust Company to reopen. The city had just one remaining bank, Florida National Bank, controlled by the wealthy du Pont interests and unlikely to fail.

The void did not last long, even in the depths of the Depression; local businessmen saw an opportunity and opened the First National Bank of Orlando, which became Sun Bank and later Sun Trust. While the bank would become the largest in Orlando, its opening competed with another event being held nearby—the American Legion Walkathon was in its 480th hour at the Orlando Coliseum. The competition had begun with thirty-seven couples, but by the twentieth day, only nineteen couples were left. Other news that day showed the depths of the Depression. The school superintendent proudly announced that the schools would be able to pay the teachers and all of the bills, but he begged for residents to pay their delinquent taxes to avoid future problems.

Two local businessmen, H.M. Voorhis and Raymer F. Maguire, still had faith in Orlando and organized Florida Faith to promote local real estate. Despite the economy, there was a great deal of business activity. The bus company, which suspended service for several months, resumed operations. Sears, Roebuck and Company opened a downtown store along with Kress, Walgreens and W.T. Grant. The city launched a "Buy Now" campaign. But the problems were bigger than Orlando leaders could cure. Federal dollars were welcome, funding projects through the city. Tinker Field got new fences, and a ten-thousand-seat football stadium was built near the baseball field.

An aerial view of downtown Orlando in the 1930s. The large building in the lower left-hand corner is Memorial High School, which was torn down to make way for a hotel, and then a condominium. *Collection of the author.*

Orange Avenue in the 1930s. The building on the near right is the Woolworth store. *Florida Photographic Collection.*

The original Municipal Airport is still in operation as Orlando Executive Airport. When this photo was taken in the 1930s, it sat in an isolated area. Today, it is surrounded by development and the busiest highways in Orlando. *Historical Society of Central Florida, Incorporated.*

There was one strange scheme to help the local economy by moving the capital from Tallahassee to Orlando. In 1933, the *Orlando Sunday Sentinel* published a full-page editorial urging the move, saying, "All that is required to switch capitals is a constitutional amendment. To bring about such an amendment, as shall presently be seen, is not an involved matter. Only political bicker can prevent such an amendment for as Orlando's good Mayor—Sam Way—declares, 'I think 75 percent of the people of Florida would be glad to see the capital moved to Orlando.'"

It was one of a number of attempts that cropped up every few years, and like all the others, it failed.

By 1936, the economy was looking up. Bank deposits rose, automobile sales increased and retail sales started going in the right direction. Orlando got its first Howard Johnson restaurant and its first Publix Super Market. The population growth slowed during the Great Depression, but the county still grew by 50 percent to 70, 074 on the eve of World War II. The Orlando population grew from 3,894 in 1910 to 9,282 in 1920; 27,330 in 1930; and 36,736 in 1940.

By 1940, Orlando was based on a citrus economy, and the price of citrus land was increasing rapidly. By the mid-1950s, the Orlando area was producing 40 percent of the state's orange crop. The coming of Walt Disney World and some crippling freezes in the 1980s reduced the importance of citrus. By 1990, the 40 percent number had fallen to just 6 percent.

The year 1940 proved to have greater significance than anyone could foresee. Social Security changed retirement, and Florida was the primary beneficiary. The first checks went to just 2,500 recipients in Florida—about the same number as in Delaware, but within three decades, millions of Florida residents would be receiving Social Security checks. The warm weather was a draw, but the lower cost of living proved to be the greatest attraction.

Chapter 15

WORLD WAR II

The other important change in the Orlando economy came from the military and the space program. In 1940, as the nation began to ramp up for possible entry into World War II, the city's municipal airport, located near downtown, became a training facility. A second airstrip was built south of downtown in 1941, and thousands of airmen trained in Orlando. Even before the United States entered World War II, Florida had become a training center for British pilots. The warm weather and large expanses of empty land made it perfect for year-round training. The Pine Castle airbase eventually replaced the city's municipal airport.

The airport was named for Colonel Mike McCoy, who died when his plane imploded and crashed while flying over Orlando. While the official name is Orlando International Airport, the luggage tags passengers receive are stamped MCO for Mike McCoy.

Before World War II, there were eight military bases in Florida; at the end of the war, there were 172. Camp Blanding in North Florida became the fourth-largest city in the state during the war. Hundreds of thousands of soldiers, sailors and pilots came for training. John Kennedy and George H.W. Bush underwent training in Florida. The impact extended far beyond the war. Thousands of the soldiers and sailors came back to live when the war was over, and thousands more made a note to retire to Florida.

On August 6, 1945, Thomas Ferebee pushed a button at 9:15 a.m. on board a B-29 and sent an atomic bomb on its way toward Hiroshima, ushering in the atomic age. In 1970, Ferebee retired from the air force and

During World War II, the air base became a major economic force, and after World War II it became Orlando International Airport. *Historical Society of Central Florida, Incorporated.*

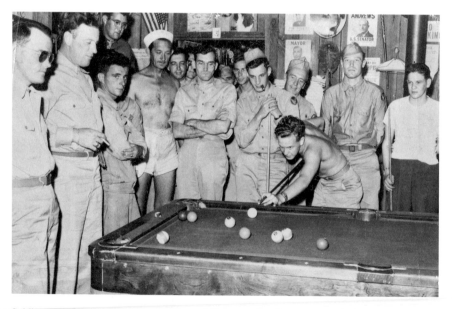

Soldiers stated at the Orlando Air Base took time to relax. Some returned when the war ended, and others came back when they retired. *Historical Society of Central Florida, Incorporated.*

Prisoners of War

WHEN THE UNITED STATES ENTERED WORLD WAR II, *the first question was where to start. The Allies were not ready for a direct assault on Europe and chose to start in Africa. At first it was rough going, but as the soldiers became battle tested, victory followed victory.*

One problem for the Allies was what to do with German prisoners of war captured in North Africa. The Sahara Desert obviously would not work, and England was overrun with people from dozens of different countries.

The decision was made to set up prisoner-of-war camps in the United States. In all, there were 340,407 German POWs housed in 480 camps. Florida became the temporary home for 11,746 Germans. The largest Florida camp was at Camp Blanding in North Florida. There were 830 German prisoners held at the Orlando airfield, and a branch camp was set up in West Orange County. A camp was also set up in Lake County and became the site for Lake-Sumter Community College after the war.

The inmates could work outside the camp to earn some spending money, and some took jobs picking oranges in Winter Garden or working in a downtown Orlando laundry. Because of the war, there was a chronic shortage of workers, especially for industries such as citrus and laundries. The POWs could not work in war-related industries or with military equipment.

One American wrote to his congressman complaining that a Nazi soldier was working in an Orlando laundry next to patriotic American women. As the war dragged on, the makeup of the prisoners changed. Those captured early in the war tended to remain very patriotic, while those captured later were less patriotic. Often there were fights between the two groups.

When the war ended, the soldiers were sent back to Europe, although many took more than a year to get back to Germany. Some had enjoyed their time in Orlando and wanted to return after the war. Under the Displaced Persons Act, they could apply to return to the United States, if they could find a sponsor in the United States. One POW, Friedrich Hayen, wrote to M. C. Britt, a Winter Garden grower, asking Britt to sponsor him as a citrus worker.

spent the final thirty years of his life in Windermere, working in his garden and fishing on Lake Down.

A week after Ferebee pushed the button, Orlando celebrated the end of World War II. People drove their cars up and down Orange Avenue with horns honking and yelling.

When the shooting stopped, the local airfields were placed on inactive status, but the start of the Cold War brought them back to active duty. The Korean War led to more expansion, and more military dollars poured into the local economy.

Pine Hills

PINE HILLS WAS DEVELOPER GORDON BARNETT'S DREAM. *As World War II came to a close, Barnett looked into the future and saw that Orlando would grow, and the new residents would need houses. His idea was to create the first suburb for Orlando. He bought land near what was then known as Robertsonville, named for Percy Robertson, whose family had settled there.*

Barnett bought 2,200 acres for fifty dollars an acre. At the time, the area was isolated and hard to reach, requiring a roundabout route. His idea was to build housing for workingmen and women, low-cost homes he initially branded Orlando Hills. But when he opened a nine-hole golf course in 1947, he changed the name to Pine Hills.

The state gave him a major boost, extending and expanding Route 50, which made Pine Hills a short ten-minute drive from downtown Orlando. In December 1952, Pine Hills was formally dedicated with three hundred completed homes, a drive-in theater and a shopping center under construction.

Although Pine Hills was designed initially to serve those who worked in downtown Orlando, it proved to be attractive to the employees of the Glenn Martin Company who arrived in the late 1950s. It was an upper-middle-class neighborhood with a country club.

There was talk of incorporating as a city and talk of annexation by Orlando, but Pine Hills remained unincorporated. Upscale motels were built, and a large Montgomery Ward department store opened. In the mid-1960s, Walt Disney stayed in Pine Hills when he came to examine land for a new theme park. In 1965, voters in Pine Hills voted against both incorporation and annexation. In retrospect, it was the beginning of a slow decline for the once-promising area.

By 1970, Pine Hills had sixteen thousand residents and, by 2010, nearly sixty thousand. But the area is not what Gordon Barnett imagined. The country club was closed and apartment complexes built there, the shopping center lost many of its tenants and the Montgomery Ward store closed. Although housing prices were exploding in other areas around Orlando, prices in Pine Hills began to level off and even decline. Much of the property became rental or government subsidized, and crime increased dramatically.

One out of seven homes was empty by 2010, and the poverty rate in Pine Hills was higher than the state average. The growth went elsewhere, and Pine Hills declined.

McCoy Air Force Base was expanded to accommodate B-47 jet bombers, and a third runway was added. City leaders realized that the downtown airport would not be able to handle the growing demand of airlines.

The city negotiated an unusual deal with the air force: the city and the military would share the base. The city built a terminal, and in late 1961, Delta Airlines inaugurated service from the new airport with a flight from Orlando to Los Angeles. The following year, Eastern Airlines began service at the new airport. As late as 1965, commercial flights continued to use the municipal airport—renamed Herndon Airport—when the air force turned over all of McCoy to the city. In 1968, a long-term lease was signed, and the city paid one dollar for what became Orlando International Airport.

Chapter 16

A COOL BREEZE AND BUG SPRAY

The railroad, the automobile and the highways did their part in opening up Orlando, but the scorching summers still kept many away and made it uncomfortable for residents. As one newspaper columnist wrote, "Can you conceive a Walt Disney World in the 95-degree summers of central Florida without air-conditioned hotels, attractions, and shops."

The tourists who began coming to Orlando after 1900 usually came for "the season," the period from early December to late March. When warm weather returned, they headed north for the summer. For year-round residents, the heat was a fact of life. It meant houses were built with high ceilings and large windows so air would flow through the home to reduce the oppressive heat.

Orlando residents would wake up in the middle of the night to find their sheets and nightclothes soaked with sweat. It was common for half-awake children and adults to change the sheets in the middle of the night. In an era before washing machines were common, the large laundries cleaned the sheets daily.

Air conditioning began in Florida in the 1830s when a North Florida doctor named John Gorrie began experimenting with air forced over ice to comfort his patients. By 1851, he had patented the first ice-making machine but was greeted mostly by scorn and tremendous resistance from the well-entrenched companies in the North that carved ice from frozen lakes and shipped it. One newspaper columnist wrote, "A crank down in Florida thinks he can make ice as good as Almighty God." Gorrie died broke and in obscurity, although he was later honored with a statue in the U.S. Capitol.

As early as 1902, the Sears Roebuck Catalog offered an electric fan for ten dollars, which could be a week's pay for many Orlando workers. A few years later, a young engineer coined the term "air conditioning" and began installing systems in textile mills and tobacco factories. Willis Carrier, the father of modern air conditioning, worked to make it more practical and versatile. In 1939, he perfected a system for high-rise buildings and began installing systems in trains and department stores. In the 1930s, movie theaters began installing air conditioning. Theaters such as the Beecham in downtown Orlando often featured signs touting air conditioning as large or larger as the signs announcing the movie. At the same time, the S.S. Kresge store on Orange Avenue was air conditioned, although most stores in Orlando would not get air conditioning until after World War II.

Room air conditioners came to Orlando in 1929 but were available only to the wealthiest homeowners. It was not until after World War II that air conditioning revolutionized Orlando. The room air conditioner became practical—if not entirely affordable when the war ended. In 1947, only a few thousand were sold in Florida, but when a less expensive model appeared in 1951, sales soared. Between 1955 and 1980, the percentage of homes with air conditioning increased from 20 percent to 80 percent.

In the 1950s, practical air conditioning units appeared in automobiles, starting with the luxury cars Packard, Cadillac and the Chrysler Imperial. But it was out of the price range of all but the wealthiest people. By 1955, 10 percent of new cars had factory-installed air conditioning; a decade later it increased to 25 percent and by 1973 was at 80 percent.

The impact was felt in Orlando. Tourists could come year-round and stay in cool hotel rooms. For residents, laundry time was cut in half, it was no longer necessary to leave windows wide open and cleaning time was reduced. Surveys found people slept longer and even their diet changed. There were more hot meals, which cooks had avoided making in the sweltering heat.

But the biggest change was to home construction. Air conditioning meant developers could put up small cinderblock houses with small windows, perfect for the thousands of retirees who were moving to the state and young couples starting out. The houses were inexpensive, often built on land that was virtually worthless a few years earlier.

Air conditioning did its part to bring more people to Orlando, but there was still one problem to be solved—although the solution may have been worse than the problem. During the summer months, Orlando endured mosquitoes that seemed to swarm everywhere.

Gatorland opened in 1949 and, in the days before Disney World, was the major attraction. Founded by Owen Goodwin, it is still owned by his family. Unlike some parks, such as Cypress Gardens, which were put out of business by Disney, Gatorland has adapted and remains popular. *Florida Photographic Collection.*

On August 6, 1945, the United States dropped the atomic bomb on Hiroshima. That morning, readers of the *Orlando Morning Sentinel* saw a front-page story about a development that would help the city grow: DDT.

DDT, short for dichlorodiphenyltrichloroethane, traces its development back to Europe in 1874. It could be used for a variety of purposes, from stamping out mosquito-borne malaria to controlling typhus-carrying lice on concentration-camp survivors.

Near the end of the war, the United States wanted to see if DDT could be used against agricultural pests and chose Orlando for the tests. The city's Livingston Street Experimental Station in downtown Orlando had been experimenting with DDT, and it was natural for the Agriculture Department to have more work done there.

Researchers fanned out across the county for ten days to treat more than fourteen thousand cows. The DDT worked, the horn flies that plagued the cows died and there was a surprise—it killed roaches. One rancher found a "bushel of dead roaches" in one of the barns that was sprayed.

DDT seemed like a miracle solution. Orlando officials asked the government for a supply of the chemical to spray in restaurants to control bugs—never knowing what the chemical might be doing to the restaurant food and the customers.

It worked on horn flies and roaches, but what about the biggest problem: mosquitoes? The *Orlando Reporter-Star* called DDT the "new wonder insecticide" and urged it be used on mosquitoes. Senator Claude Pepper was clearly overjoyed: "Today Orlando is the scene of a series of experiments which may eventually develop a method for the complete extermination of some of man's ancient plagues."

Ray Charles in Orlando

IN 1945, RAY CHARLES PACKED A SMALL STEAMER TRUNK. *He had two pairs of pants, two shirts, tennis shoes, underwear and a clarinet—all hand-me-downs. He had two dollars in his pocket, was fifteen years old and had just learned that his thirty-two-year-old mother had died. He was setting off into a world he could not see. Since the age of seven, he had been blind and a student at the state school for the blind in St. Augustine.*

His first stop was Jacksonville, where he played in some clubs and stayed with his aunt. In 1946, he met bandleader Tiny York, who scheduled appearances in Central Florida. The tour fell apart, and Charles was stranded and broke in Orlando. Charles remained in Orlando for eight months, scratching to make ends meet. "You pray to God you will be able to make the payment," he said. When he could not pay his landlady, she let him stay anyway.

There were several clubs for African Americans, including the Sunshine Club, the Casino and the Quarterback Club. He played regularly but not constantly, and sometimes he went two days without eating. He picked up jobs playing in the black clubs in small towns outside Orlando like DeLand and Kissimmee.

Sometimes he would play, but there would be no pay. "Sometimes you'd work in these places and don't get paid," he recalled years later. Despite this, he did save enough money to purchase his first luxury item, a seventy-eight-rpm record player. He played a few white clubs in Orlando—not the music he wanted to play—but the tips were good.

The big band era was coming to an end, and work was tougher to find. "I could have lived there if the work had been there. But the jobs began to dry up, nobody hiring nobody. Eventually the picking just got too thin around Orlando. There just wasn't no work."

Eventually he asked a friend to look at a map and find the city as far away from Florida as possible. He headed to Seattle.

Mosquitoes were a deterrent to summer tourism and to attracting permanent residents. Now, DDT could control them. Soon, trucks loaded with DDT were driving through Orlando spraying clouds of the deadly chemical. Without realizing the ecological damage the chemical was causing, residents welcomed the trucks and even called city officials asking that the trucks be sent by more often.

In 1962, author Rachel Carson warned of the dangers of DDT in her classic book, *Silent Spring*, and a decade later, the federal government banned the substance.

The long-range implications were serious, but it helped bring tourists and new residents to Orlando.

Chapter 17

THE SPACE RACE

In 1950, the space program came to nearby Cape Canaveral. During World War II, the United States launched test rockets at White Sands Proving Ground in New Mexico. But there were problems with the site: it was too confined, and if a rocket failed, it could hit populated areas. The search for other sites led to El Centro, California, but this time it was Mexico that objected; errant rockets could end up striking in Mexico.

The government realized that the site would have to be on the water so that failed shots would land harmlessly in the ocean. Scientists found that being closer to the equator made launches easier.

The choice was the Banana River Naval Air Station near Titusville. In 1949, President Harry Truman authorized a testing facility there, later renamed Patrick Air Force Base for air force general Mason Patrick.

In July 1950, the first missile was launched, a V-2 rocket confiscated from the Germans and a WAC corporal rocket put together for the test. Both American and German scientists worked on the launch. The military operated the base until 1958, and then the National Aeronautics and Space Administration (NASA) took over. Thousands of additional acres were added, and the center became more crucial when President John Kennedy announced his determination to put a man on the moon in the 1960s.

Following Kennedy's assassination in 1963, President Lyndon Johnson ordered Cape Canaveral renamed Cape Kennedy. Both the military base and the nearby community initially became Cape Kennedy, but residents of the community did not like the change and took back the name Cape Canaveral.

IN 1926, AT THE HEIGHT *of the land boom, city leaders agreed to spend $175,000 to build a municipal auditorium. The old opera house had been torn down, and theaters such as the Beacham had become movie houses and the city needed a performance hall.*

The hall opened in 1927 with a performance by the LaScala Grand Opera Company of Philadelphia. It featured a range of productions and even showed movies. A favorite were the country music concerts that came through town frequently.

Elvis Presley kisses *Sentinel* reporter Jean Yothers after a performance in Orlando in 1956. Yothers later directed the Orange County History Museum. *Orlando Sentinel.*

One of those tours brought a musical phenomenon. It was 1955, and a young singer named Elvis Presley was performing at the city's Municipal Auditorium. He was still a year away from his breakthrough performances on **The Ed Sullivan Show** *and had not yet scored a top-ten hit. That did not matter to the teenage girls who packed the auditorium.*

Presley was performing with Hank Snow's All-Star Jamboree—the first of his three appearances in Orlando within a year. Hank Snow, the legendary country singer had assembled a first-rate tour, including Faron Young, who had his first number one hit, "Live Fast, Love Hard, Die Young." Snow himself had five top ten songs that year. Slim Whitman had a number of hits and was a big draw. Although the term "country music," was coming in vogue, newspapers still referred to it as "hillbilly" music.

Many in the crowd had come to see Presley, who was being paid fifty dollars a show. When Snow came out to start the show, the crowd chanted for Presley. In a misguided effort to quiet the crowd, the announcer explained that Presley was not even in the building— he was outside signing autographs. It was the wrong thing to say, as many in the crowd streamed outside to find Elvis.

The Municipal Auditorium was not air conditioned until 1962, and people joked that it was like a Turkish bath.

Presley came back in July, and this time it was Andy Griffith who was the headliner. Griffith had appeared on Broadway, had a hit record joking about football and was a singer. Marty Robbins was also on the bill, although he was little known at the time.

Elvis returned a third time in August 1956, and a lot had changed. This time he was big news and a headliner. The local newspaper had the story on the front page: "Wiggling Elvis to Play Orlando Twice Today." He now had two hit songs, "Hound Dog" and "Don't Be Cruel," and had appeared on national television programs hosted by Steve Allen and Milton Berle. For this Orlando concert, he wore an orange sport coat. Orlando Morning Sentinel *reporter Jean Yothers interviewed him, admired his blue-lace shirt, and got a kiss.*

A month later, Presley was on the Sullivan show and quickly became the king of rock and roll. He returned to Orlando in 1977 to perform just six months before he died.

The base was about thirty miles from Orlando, the largest city in the area. Many of the military contractors who did business at the cape set up their offices in Orlando, and many of the workers at the cape chose to live in Orlando, where their spouses often found work.

The cape had the space program, but Orlando had the major airport. It meant a boon for Orlando and continues to fuel many of the high-tech companies and military contractors that initially came because of the space program.

The significance of the cape came in 1957 when Americans heard the news that the Russians had sent the satellite Sputnik into space. The space race was on, and Central Florida was at the center of it. In 1961, President John Kennedy announced that the United States would put a man on the moon by the end of the decade. Orlando would be a beneficiary of the billions of dollars spent on the space program. Orlando had called itself the City Beautiful for decades, but now it was changed to "Action Center of Florida," a slogan that never caught on.

In 1956, the Glenn L. Martin Company, builder of the Matador Missile, purchased twelve square miles near Orlando for $2 million and built an $18 million plant. It set off a land boom not seen since the 1920s. Land near the plant, which had been selling for $200 an acre, soared overnight to over $1,000 an acre. The Martin Company bought more than seven thousand acres and eventually became Lockheed-Martin and attracted scores of other military-related companies. Martin moved its scientists and engineers from Maryland and eventually became the city's largest employer, with nearly eight thousand workers. But just as importantly, other related businesses came to Orlando to be near the Martin plant. By the 1970s, more than seventy such businesses were in Orlando. The

A Corporate Coup

Bonnie Wise was the driving force behind the Tupperware headquarters in Orlando. It was Orlando's first national company. *Collection of Bob Kealing*

MARTIN WAS NOT *the first company to move a major part of its operations to Orlando. The first major national company to move major operations to Orlando was Tupperware. It is hard to imagine a stranger series of circumstances that brought Tupperware to Orlando. Earl Tupper had created not only the plastic products that caught the fancy of the nation but also created a home-party system for selling the airtight bowls.*

Tupper's original plan was to build a headquarters in Cuero, Texas, utilizing an old military base. At first, the town seemed to welcome Tupper, but gradually the residents of the small town—known for its turkeys—began to whisper that it was a bad deal for Cuero. Perhaps there was oil under the base, the locals speculated. Tupper dropped Cuero and began searching for a new headquarters.

Meanwhile, there were huge problems with his sales and distribution systems, and a South Florida distributor named Bonnie Wise called Tupper to complain. She impressed him with her bluntness, and soon she became head of Tupperware Home Parties Division. Wise was working in Florida and pushed for the new headquarters to be located there.

Tupper considered various Florida sites, including Miami, Jupiter, Boca Raton, and even Starke, the home of the state penitentiary. In 1951, Tupper became interested in Orlando, but Wise kept pushing for a location that was more glamorous. She tried to discourage Tupper, telling him, "I honestly think you could be terribly disappointed."

Tupper found nearly a thousand acres for sale between Orlando and Kissimmee. He bought it from the legendary Bronson family, one of the state's largest cattle owners.

Not only was the company a significant coup for Orlando, but Tupperware also held sales conferences each year, bringing in hundreds of distributors from throughout the country. They often stayed for a few days to enjoy the warm weather.

As for Wise, she was instrumental in turning Tupperware into a major success, and her fame grew. She appeared on the cover of Business Week in 1954, but she clashed repeatedly with Tupper, and in 1958, he fired her, leaving her with nothing.

The headquarters featured a number of large auditoriums, which often featured concerts for Orlando and Kissimmee residents.

The coming of the Martin plant in the 1950s brought thousands of jobs and helped attract other defense-related companies to Orlando. *Florida Photographic Collection.*

success of Martin led city officials to go after more light industry, and five office parks were established.

The arrival of the Martin Company also had an impact on Sun Bank. Two Martin executives came to Orlando to scout possible sites for their plant. They told no one they were coming, and they stopped at a local bank to inquire about bank services. They received an icy reception and walked down the street to Sun Bank. There, they received a warm welcome and introductions to some of the major people in Orlando. With the help of Sun Bank, Martin acquired the property and made arrangements for new roads and utility lines and even a guarantee of a sewage system—all within twenty-two days.

Chapter 18

THE SHOPPING SPREE

The new Martin employees had money to spend, and developers responded by building the town's first shopping centers, one in Pine Hills and the second just outside downtown Orlando called Colonial Plaza.

By today's standards, Colonial Plaza was little more than a strip mall: a Walgreens Drug Store, a Publix Super Market, a Woolworth store, the iconic Ronnie's restaurant, smaller shops and a Belk-Lindsay Department Store. When it opened in 1956, it revolutionized shopping in Orlando.

For nearly a century, a small stretch of downtown Orlando was the shopping center of the town. There were originally two local department stores downtown, large brick buildings sitting across from one another and competing for decades.

The Yowell-Duckworth store opened in 1914 in a new four-story building. A fifth floor was added in 1919. Duckworth sold his interest to Eugene Drew, and the store was renamed Yowell-Drew. In 1944, it was sold to the Ivey Company of North Carolina and renamed Yowell-Drew-Ivey, and then in 1953 it became Ivey's. Ivey's closed the downtown store in 1976 to concentrate on suburban malls.

Across Orange Avenue was Dickson-Ives, which began as a grocery store in 1896. In 1913, it became a department store while retaining the grocery business. In 1919, Dickson-Ives dropped the groceries and in 1924 moved into a new four-story building. The two department stores competed but could not see that the real competition would come from suburban malls. Dickson-Ives remodeled its store in 1960, hoping to attract more customers

Orange Avenue in the late 1950s. The block on the near right featuring a McCrory's was torn down to make way for an office building and condominium. *Florida Photographic Collection.*

downtown. The store changed owners several times, but business continued to decline. On April 11, 1965, employees were told at 11:30 a.m. to get their personal things together and be out of the building by noon. The company declared bankruptcy.

Walgreens was the first national chain to leave downtown, moving to Colonial Plaza. In 1960, Montgomery Ward, one of the world's largest retailers at the time, built a massive store in Pine Hills. Rutland's, the leading clothing store, remained downtown for a time but opened a second store in Colonial Plaza. A Sears Roebuck store and J.C. Penney store hung on but eventually closed their downtown stores to concentrate on suburban malls.

Sears moved to what became Fashion Square Mall in 1963 just two miles from its previous location in downtown Orlando. When the store opened, it sat by itself, but developers attached a mall. Initially, a Robinson's of Florida store opened in 1973 and anchored the other end of the mall. Three other department stores, including J.C. Penney moved to the mall.

Colonial Plaza was Orlando's first shopping mall and helped bring about the end of the downtown department stores. *Historical Society of Central Florida, Incorporated.*

Fashion Square was just two blocks from Colonial Plaza, setting up a major retailing battle. Unfortunately, Colonial Plaza was at a disadvantage. Because of its original shape, it was difficult to add onto the mall. Jordan Marsh had originally planned on building a massive store downtown, but the property owner tried to raise the price at the last minute, and the store went to Colonial Plaza instead. When the five-story Jordan Marsh Department Store opened in 1962, Colonial Plaza became T-shaped, with some of the stores outside and some inside. A second addition extended the Jordan Marsh wing, putting the store in the middle of the addition. Belk-Lindsay moved to the other end of the mall, and shoppers had to pass through Jordan Marsh to get to Belk-Lindsay and the other stores.

Jordan Marsh quickly became the city's leading upscale department store. For many, Jordan Marsh offered a thrill ride, four floors of escalators in a city that had never seen more than two floors of escalators. On the day the store opened, the store stationed stewardesses and pilots from Eastern Airlines to instruct people on how to ride the escalators and hand them toy Eastern Airline pilot wings.

As the downtown stores had done, the Fashion Square and Colonial Plaza stores faced competition from newer, bigger malls. Altamonte Mall opened

Kerouac's Home

Jack Kerouac was on the verge of fame when he moved to Orlando to be near his mother and sister. Two months after arriving, his classic book *On the Road* was published. He wrote in the back room of his College Park home. *Historical Society of Central Florida, Incorporated.*

JACK KEROUAC ARRIVED IN ORLANDO *in 1956 after a twenty-four-hour bus ride from New York. He was a virtual unknown, but within a few months he would become one of the best-known writers in the country. He had come to Orlando at the request of his mother, who wanted the family to be together.*

Two months after his arrival, his classic On the Road *was published and brought him instant fame. He wrote the book five years earlier but struggled to find a publisher. He and his mother rented a small apartment in back of a house in College Park. Sitting in the back room of the ramshackle house, he wrote* The Dharma Bums, *which did not come close to the success of* On the Road. *He returned to New York, and then back to Orlando, this time settling in a suburban house where he wrote* Big Sur.

He bought land and planned to build a compound for his mother, sister, brother-in-law and himself. But as with so many things in his life, this was never materialized. He turned to drinking and struggled to pay his bills despite his fame.

He moved to Massachusetts, but his mother urged him to return to Florida, and this time he chose St. Petersburg, where he died at the age of forty-seven.

Today, the house where he wrote in College Park has been turned into a residence for visiting writers. The back room where he wrote is just as he left it, the typewriter sitting ready with his trademark yellow paper.

ON SEPTEMBER 7, 1960, *readers of the* Orlando Morning Sentinel *awoke to the news that Hurricane Donna had raked Puerto Rico, leaving more than 102 people dead. The newspaper carried the usual warning that people in Orlando should be prepared in case the storm headed toward Central Florida.*

Most people shrugged off the warning. The last hurricane to come toward Orlando was in 1949, and by the time it arrived, it was downgraded to a tropical storm. Few people in Orlando had ever experienced a hurricane.

Donna left Puerto Rico and headed toward the Bahamas and then hit Miami with winds up to 150 miles per hour. The weather was already miserable in Orlando;

Orlando had never seen anything as bad as Hurricane Donna when it struck in 1960. The winds did some damage, but it was the pounding rain that cause the most destruction. *Historical Society of Central Florida, Incorporated.*

a weak pressure system unrelated to the hurricane dumped three inches of rain on the city, soaking the ground and filling the lakes.

On September 8, local officials began to sound the alarm: Donna was a huge storm. People began to move into shelters. It hit Orlando with fifty-mile-per-hour winds, with gusts at seventy-three miles per hour. The more than four inches of rain, combined with the already swollen lakes and soggy ground, caused flooding all over town. Falling trees knocked down power lines, and thousands of people lost power. Schools closed for three days, and flooding was ankle- to knee-deep in many parts of the city.

Until 2004, it would be remembered as the worst storm to hit Orlando.

in 1973, followed by the giant Florida Mall in 1986. Jordan Marsh closed its Orlando stores in 1991. An Ivey's was built in front of Colonial Plaza, but it did not help.

At Colonial Plaza, the huge Jordan Marsh building sat empty. The mall owners built wooden walls so that shoppers passed through the former department store surrounded by plywood panels. The mall became a ghost town, with empty storefronts outnumbering the remaining businesses.

In 1994, developers bought the mall and announced plans to tear down most of it and build what was called a power mall, a collection of major stores with some smaller shops mixed in. Instead of an enclosed mall, the new mall was open, and stores were spread out. Little was left of the mall that had changed shopping forever in Orlando.

In 2002, the Mall at Millenia opened, giving Orlando shoppers a new set of shopping choices, including Neiman-Marcus and Bloomingdale's. It, along with Florida Mall, became a major destination for foreign shoppers— especially from Latin America—who flocked to Orlando for the theme parks and the shopping.

As the stores moved out of downtown, some businesses remained and some built new buildings. The *Sentinel-Star* built a massive new building on Orange Avenue, a new hotel went up on Lake Eola and other buildings expanded.

Also bringing change to Orlando was a massive road-building program. The Sunshine State Parkway, later named Florida's Turnpike and now the Ronald Regan Turnpike, opened in 1963, connecting Orlando to I-75 in the north and to South Florida through Fort Pierce. In 1965, I-4 was completed between Daytona Beach and Tampa. One more transportation link would complete the highway network. If Orlando was to serve the space coast, it had to be easier to reach. City leaders responded with an expressway to make getting to Cape Canaveral easier. Orlando was the hub of a highway system reaching out in all directions.

Chapter 19

BUILDING A UNIVERSITY

B y the mid-1950s, the state was facing some scary numbers. Florida demographers looked into the future and found the state was totally unprepared to provide a college education to high school graduates. State demographers figured that by 1975, there would be 125,000 high school seniors applying to the state's three universities, the University of Florida, Florida State and Florida A&M University.

The state launched a sweeping program to increase the number of universities, beginning with the University of South Florida in 1956. It determined that a school was needed for Central Florida, and Orlando leaders began lobbying for the school to be built there. At first, they wanted a branch campus of the University of Florida or perhaps a graduate school. Eventually, they began pushing for a four-year college they could call their own.

They referred to it as a "space university," hoping that the nation's love affair with the Mercury Program and the astronauts would help their cause. Sun Bank president Billy Dial began using his considerable influence, and in 1963, the legislation was signed to create a four-year school—known initially as the New State University in Central Florida until a permanent name could be chosen.

The legislature was vague about where the new school should be located. The area the new school was to serve spread from Flagler County, north of Daytona Beach to Fort Pierce in the South, and could be in any of nine counties. There was some thought that it should be in Brevard County, site of the growing space program and a great location for a school whose primary interest was technology.

When construction began in the 1960s, Florida Technological University was short of money and could only build a limited number of buildings. *University of Central Florida Archives.*

Orlando leaders were not about to let the school get away. While the other counties did little or nothing, leaders in Orlando moved into action. They considered three sites, one on the South Orange Blossom Trail, a second in Seminole County, and a third east of Orlando. The third site was especially attractive because it was just thirty miles from Cape Kennedy and could serve students from the space center.

State officials could not agree. The State Board of Control deadlocked repeatedly. The South Orlando site was near the Martin plant, with its hundreds of engineers and high-tech facilities. The Seminole County site was in Tuskawilla. A series of tie votes delayed the process. Finally, the

University of Central Florida president John Hitt and former president Bill Clinton at the graduation ceremony marking the school's fiftieth anniversary in 2013. *University of Central Florida.*

board voted 5–1 to buy the East Orange site, land owned by New Jersey contractor Frank Adamucci. Adamucci had agreed to donate 500 acres if the state would pay $1,000 an acre for the other 500 acres he owned. Other acquisitions increased the site to 1,227 acres.

While the state agreed to buy the land, no money was appropriated. The state wanted Orange County to come up with the cash, and then be repaid by the state. But the county said it did not have the money. In early 1965, eighty-nine local residents put up a million dollars to buy the land. The contributors were told they would get the money back, but it depended on the always unpredictable legislature.

But funding to actually build the campus faced an uncertain future in the legislature. That is when a long shot by attorney Charles Gray paid off for Orlando. In the 1964 gubernatorial contest, Gray backed Jacksonville mayor Haydon Burns, who seemed to have the least chance among the six Democratic candidates. In an upset, Burns won and was indebted to Gray. Gray's top request was that the legislature move on the university for Orlando, and Burns put the UCF project to the top of his funding requests.

Orlando got what would one day become the nation's second-largest university. Frank Adamucci did not get to enjoy his $500,000. In August 1965, Adamucci was shot to death in his Cherry Hill, New Jersey motel. The man who shot him testified that he had gone to the motel to collect some money, but a fight ensued, and as the two wrestled over a gun, it went off, killing Adamucci. Law enforcement officials still believe that the murder was mob related.

Orlando had legislative approval and a large empty tract of land east of town, but not much else. The legislature promised $11 million for construction to build a school for 1,500 students to open in 1968 but only came up with $7 million. It meant that the early classroom buildings served a number of purposes, rather than being dedicated to a single area. Even the library became a multipurpose building, with a bookstore in the basement. It also meant that the school was always behind when it came to building classrooms and parking facilities.

Dr. Charles Millican, the dean of the University of South Florida School of Business, became the first president. He was an excellent choice, making decisions about the design of the campus that would serve the school for decades to come and making it clear that the new school would focus on the student—what he called "accent on the individual."

Local officials pushed the idea of a "space university," dedicated to new technology, but when approval came, they backed off the technology emphasis. Dial, who had successfully lobbied the legislature, now said the school needed to stress a number of areas, including liberal arts. But the *Orlando Sentinel Star* continued to push for a name that reflected the "space university." It looked like the *Sentinel* had lost when a local committee recommended three possible names: University of Central Florida, Florida Central University and Central Florida University. But the Florida Board of Regents rejected all three and went with the technology-related name: Florida Technological University. A dozen years later, it became the University of Central Florida.

The university's first mascot was "Citronaut," a cartoonish mix between an orange and an astronaut that was instantly unpopular. A nurse at the school's health center suggested "Vincent the Vulture" as a mascot until the students selected the Knight of Pegasus as the mascot.

From the beginning, the university was always short of money. Rising energy prices and inflation took their toll in the 1970s. The school shut down for ten days in 1974 and again for two weeks in 1976 to save money. "Pure and simple, FTU does not have the money needed to operate," Millican said.

Millican served as president until 1978 when Trevor Colbourn took over. A native of Australia, Colbourn was vice president and acting president at San Diego State University. It was Colbourn who pulled Florida Technological University away from its technological emphasis and pushed to have the school renamed. He created the honors program, opened a research park, launched satellite campuses and started the university's football team. During his eleven years as president, he saw enrollment increase by 75 percent to over eighteen thousand. He more than doubled the number of buildings on campus, but still construction was far behind what was needed.

He started a football team in 1979, with a coaching staff consisting entirely of volunteers. There was no locker room, and players were responsible for washing their own uniforms. The team began in Division III, playing St. Leo College in its first game—a 21–0 victory. Lou Saban became coach in 1982, and the school moved to Division II. But despite his heady background in the National Football League with the Buffalo Bills and Boston Patriots, Saban was a disaster. His team went 5–6 in his second season when he resigned. Saban left it in financial disarray. There was talk of disbanding the team, but some fundraisers—actor Burt Reynolds helped out—saved football at UCF.

Gene McDowell took over as head coach after a successful stint as an assistant coach at Florida State. With the gift of some old uniforms and equipment from FSU, McDowell was able to keep the program going. He coached for thirteen years and took the program to the NCAA 1-AA level.

When Colbourn stepped down in 1989, Steven Altman, who had been president of Texas A&I University-Kingsville (now Texas A&M University-Kingsville), and the author of numerous books on management, became president. His tenure lasted less than two years. Altman became embroiled in a scandal involving escorts that started when the Florida Department of Law Enforcement investigated prostitution in Tallahassee. Altman utilized an escort service linked to prostitution although he denied it was for anything more than a massage. *Orlando Sentinel* reporter Lauren Richie examined a number of Altman's expense accounts and found he had called escort services in Tampa, Miami, Atlanta and Washington, D.C., while on university business. Altman was forced out.

UCF had an interim president until John C. Hitt was selected as the school's fourth president. After stints at Texas Christian University and

The Fish Loan

Gary's Duck Inn on Orange Blossom Trail was a local favorite and the inspiration for Red Lobster. *Darden Restaurants.*

JOE LEE REMEMBERS THE FIRST TIME HE SAW ORLANDO: *it was 1967, and he was driving through with his friend and mentor, Bill Darden. They were on their way to Lakeland, Florida, to open a new restaurant called Red Lobster. Lee said he remembers the orange groves and the sweet smell of the blossoms. It was before the opening of Disney World, and citrus was still the dominant industry in the area.*

Darden had already established himself in Georgia with several restaurants and then invested in an Orlando landmark, Gary's Duck Inn, which was a favorite of both local residents and tourists who drove along the Orange Blossom Trail in the days before interstate highways and the Florida turnpike.

Lee wanted to learn the restaurant business and hoped to observe Darden in action and then open his own restaurant. Instead, Darden offered Lee a job, and the two created the largest casual dining chain in the nation with $8 billion in sales in 2012.

Darden planned to create a casual dining seafood restaurant on Interstate 4 between Orlando and Tampa. Lakeland was chosen because it was inland, away from the seafood restaurants that lined the coast, and Lakeland was easily reached by trucks bringing fresh fish from both the Atlantic Ocean and the Gulf of Mexico.

The concept they created became known as casual dining. The restaurant in Lakeland was an immediate success, and the two began making plans to expand. With multiple restaurants, they needed a company headquarters, and Darden chose Orlando. Lee said the news that the arrival of Disney World would mean expansion of the Orlando airport and easy access throughout the Southeast—neither Darden nor Lee saw Red Lobster expanding beyond the South—led them to pick Orlando.

They set up a credit line with the First National Bank of Orlando (now SunTrust) establishing what they jokingly called the bank's first "fish loan." Lee moved to Orlando in 1969 and opened Red Lobster restaurants in Orlando. It was not as easy as it had been in Lakeland. International Drive eventually drew millions of tourists each year, but at the time, it was in an isolated area. Lee recalled going over to the Martin plant each day to hand out coupons in the hope of attracting lunchtime visitors. Another location, about ten miles from downtown, was selected even though some wondered if the population would ever move that far out of town.

It did work. The company sold out to General Mills, which gave it enough money to expand, but did not fit with the company's plans. General Mills expanded it to four hundred locations and then spun it off, and Darden and Lee took control again. It became the only Fortune 500 company in Orlando. (Hughes Supply was a local Fortune 500 company until it was acquired by Home Depot.)

Orlando became the test kitchen for Darden. It tried out its first Olive Garden in 1982 before taking the concept nationwide. Two of its Orlando concepts met with mixed success. China Coast grew to fifty locations after its Orlando start but was never successful and closed in 1995. Smokey Bones began in Orlando but was sold off because it did not fit in with growth plans.

The company launched Olive Garden, Bahama Breeze and Seasons 52 and acquired Longhorn Steakhouse, Capital Grille, and other chains.

Bill Darden's idea grew to include more than 2,100 restaurants. He died in 1994, and Lee took over the company. In 2005, Lee stepped down, and Clarence Otis became president.

Otis was born in Vicksburg, Mississippi, the son of a janitor, in 1956. The family moved to Los Angeles and settled in Watts just as the civil unrest was beginning there. He graduated from Stanford Law School but found finance more attractive than law. He worked for a number of financial firms, before becoming the Darden treasurer in 1995. A decade later, he became president of the world's largest casual dining company with nearly 200,000 employees, including nearly 3,000 in the Orlando area.

Bradley, he became vice-president for academic affairs at the University of Maine and later interim president. Hitt came with an ambitious agenda.

When he took over, there were twenty thousand students—he would triple enrollment in twenty years—and the school was at a crossroads. Florida's universities were tightly controlled by the State University System of Florida and its chancellor, Charles Reed. The university presidents had little power outside of their schools, and decisions about expansion rested with the state. The system helped the University of Florida and Florida State University, which had tremendous support in the legislature, but left the other colleges to fight for scraps.

When Reed stepped down in 1998, that changed. Each college could fight for what it wanted. It was the opening Hitt was looking for. Since coming to UCF in 1992, he had stressed partnerships with local governments, companies and individuals. It allowed him to create a strong network when he began to push for things that others thought impossible. He partnered with the University of South Florida and corporations to create the High Tech Corridor, which grew into one of the region's significant economic tools.

Hitt pushed the football program, guiding it into the Mid-America Conference, then to Conference USA and finally to the Big East, which became the American Athletic Conference. Since its beginnings, the UCF football team had played its games in the city-owned stadium downtown. Having the stadium downtown gave the school a feeling that it was a commuter school—something it had dealt with since its founding. In 2007, the team opened against the Texas Longhorns in Brighthouse Stadium on the UCF campus. The stadium seats forty-five thousand and is the centerpiece for a campus expansion that includes a new field house, student housing and shops.

Hitt defied all of the odds when he began to campaign for a medical school. He faced tremendous opposition from Florida medical schools that saw the new school as competition for students, state funding, and donations. But in 2006, Hitt got approval for the medical school, and in 2013, the school graduated its first class.

Orlando is also home to Valencia College, which began as Valencia Junior College in 1967 with 581 students and twenty faculty members, then became Valencia Community College and finally Valencia College. It is a feeder school for the University of Central Florida, which each year accepts thousands of Valencia students.

Chapter 20

THE ARRIVAL OF DISNEY

The railroad, the automobile, a vast highway system, air conditioning, the space race, and the weather all played a role in the development of Orlando. But all of them together pale in comparison to the impact of Disney World.

Disneyland opened in 1955 and was an instant hit. Attendance surpassed all expectations, but the success also exposed problems. Disney was strapped for cash when he purchased the Anaheim, California land for Disneyland. Businesses, seeking to capitalize on Disneyland's success, sprung up around his park and the guests enjoying the rides could see outside the park. The atmosphere outside the park was exactly what Disney had tried to avoid inside the park. Hotels, restaurants, gift shops and other businesses had crowded around his 160 acres.

No sooner had Disneyland opened than people began asking Walt Disney when he would open a second park. He brushed off the questions, saying much more needed to be done with the original Disneyland, but he already had a second park in mind. One study showed that just 2 percent of the Disneyland visitors came from east of the Mississippi River.

In 1958, Disney studied the feasibility of building a second theme park near Secaucus, New Jersey. The study found that the park could only open four months a year and would not be profitable. Disney did not think the New York area would support the park.

St. Louis looked promising; the city was celebrating its 200th anniversary and what started out as a request for a promotional film turned into

Walt's Parents

WALT DISNEY WAS NOT THE ONLY *Disney who came to Florida with a dream, but he was far more successful than the Disneys who came before him.*

His grandfather, Kepple, and father, Elias, were Canadians who immigrated to the United States and moved to Kansas. Elias Disney met his future wife, Flora Call, but it looked like the relationship might be doomed because the Call family was leaving for Florida. Rather than give up Flora, Elias and his father decided to follow them to Florida.

They settled in the long-forgotten community of Akron, not far from Orlando. Elias and Flora married in Daytona Beach in 1888, and for a brief time, he operated a hotel there—one of the first tourist hotels in the area. He worked

Walt Disney with his mother, who lived in Paisley, north of Orlando, in the 1800s. *Disney archives.*

as a mailman before buying an eighty-acre orange grove north of Orlando in Paisley.

A freeze ruined their crop, and they had no way to make money. In 1889, Elias moved to Chicago and became a construction worker. Walt Disney was born in there in 1901. Later, the family moved to Missouri. Walt came back to Orlando in the 1960s, buying twenty-seven thousand acres of land just miles from where his father's eighty-acre orange grove had failed. Today, Walt Disney's creation fills more than 100,000 hotel rooms, just fifty miles from where his father failed to fill fewer than two dozen rooms.

serious talks about a development. Disney visited the city, and within a month, the *New York Times* reported that the city would be the site of another Disneyland—this one indoors in downtown St. Louis. But there had been no decision, and Disney gradually lost interest in the St. Louis project because he had something else in mind—something much grander than a building.

In 1959, Disney told the *Miami Herald* that he thought Florida would be better in many ways than California for a park. He was considering about six thousand acres north of Palm Beach for a planned City of Tomorrow, but that fell through.

Early in 1963, Walt Disney told a close group of associates to find five thousand to ten thousand acres in Florida. He kept pretending that St. Louis, Niagara Falls and a site outside Washington, D.C., were still in the running, but it was a ruse to draw attention from Central Florida. He flew to all three cities and then headed for his true objective, Florida. He did not want to compete with the beach for tourists, so he wanted an inland site. He arrived in Tampa on November 21 and drove from Tampa to Ocala to look at the area.

The next morning, he flew over Central Florida. Ocala was promising but did not have the road network Disney wanted. The area was familiar to Disney, who as a child had visited his aunt, who lived between Orlando and Ocala. The plane headed toward Orlando. As they flew over an area outside of town, Disney looked out the window and said, "That's it." Later he said it was the highways that attracted him, as the Interstate and the Florida Turnpike crossed just where he wanted to put his new park.

When they landed, Walt Disney was told that a few hours earlier, John Kennedy was assassinated in Dallas. Only a handful of people knew of Disney's decision, and keeping it quiet was vital to buying the land at a reasonable price.

Disney began buying twenty-seven thousand acres for an average of $200 an acre. In later years, Disney critics claimed the company underpaid for the land, but at the time, much of it was underwater, and the sellers were happy to sell it. It was far more than the company needed, but Walt always regretted not buying enough land when he built Disneyland in Anaheim, California.

Disney hired Miami attorney Paul Helliwell to acquire the land. Helliwell was a World War II spy, just the kind of cloak-and-dagger personality Disney would need to keep the land buying secret.

In 1965, Helliwell met with the president of Sun Bank, Billy Dial, and told him he represented a businessman who wanted to bring a large industry to Florida. Helliwell said the businessman was considering three sites: eastern Volusia County near Daytona Beach, Ormond Beach and a site near Orlando. Helliwell said he was pushing for the Orlando site but needed help with some land.

Using boats, Disney executives examine the land they bought for Disney World. *Florida Photographic Collection.*

Walt Disney and his brother Roy announced the coming of Disney World in 1965 at Walt's only public appearance in Orlando. Governor Haydon Burns sat between them. *Florida Photographic Collection.*

Thousands turned out for Disney's opening day in 1971, but even larger crowds soon
followed. *Orlando Sentinel.*

This 1967 front page from the *Orlando Sentinel* contained an artist's drawing of the new Disney World. It was actually Walt's dream of a utopian city, and none of it was ever built. *Orlando Sentinel.*

Using fronts, Disney purchased 12,500 acres from the Demetree cousins—land they were happy to unload. They had a $90,000 payment coming due, and there was almost nothing they could do with the land. In a strange deal, Tufts University held the mineral rights. When one landowner declined to sell, local attorney Martin Segal was asked to help convince the landowner to sell the land. Segal knew the man was a fan of Alabama football, so he went out and talked about Coach Bear Bryant for a bit and convinced the man to sell. Segal received no fee for his crucial help and had no idea he was helping Disney.

One of the enduring myths of the Disney land purchases was about who in Orlando knew what. In 1977, *Florida Trend* magazine claimed that *Orlando Sentinel* publisher Martin Andersen knew about the deal. Andersen vigorously denied he had known. The *Florida Trend* article failed to understand the nature of Andersen's role as a publisher and, more importantly, his role as a businessman. Nearly every day, people showed up at Andersen's office on Orange Avenue seeking an audience. They wanted to build something, open something, sell something, or find investors. They hoped that Andersen might run something about them in his newspaper to give them a boost, or give them advice, or perhaps even invest himself. When Helliwell showed up seeking advice on how to deal with some landowners, he was just another in the long procession. And there was Andersen the businessman, who relished land investment. When he sold the *Sentinel* to the *Chicago Tribune* in the mid-1960s, he kept the land the newspaper plant was on and later sold it to the *Tribune* for three times what the paper had fetched. If Andersen knew that Disney was buying land, he would have certainly purchased some neighboring property, as he had done in other situations. And the *Sentinel* reported the land transactions in detail, and speculated about a number of possible buyers. Because of the *Sentinel*, everyone in town knew that vast amounts of land were being purchased.

As for Sun Bank president Billy Dial, he also denied he knew about the deal until almost the very end. Dial had learned not to press those who came to his office seeking help and advice. After finishing the land purchases, Walt's brother, Roy, came to Dial's home and told him Sun Bank would handle Disney's banking in Orlando.

Disney executives took roundabout routes flying to Orlando to avoid suspicion. One executive flew through St. Louis and stopped to see his mother. When people in Orlando found out about the executive flying from St. Louis, there was instant speculation that McDonnell Aircraft was the land buyer. It did make some sense because the Martin Company already had a plant in Orlando.

While having breakfast in an Orlando motel, a waitress recognized Walt, who denied he was Walt Disney and then admitted it and asked the waitress to keep quiet about his presence in the motel. She did.

In all, Disney used nine front companies to buy the land. The layers were so thick that people actually buying the land had no idea whom they represented. The company numbered memos dealing with the new park to make sure none leaked out. Still, the denials kept coming. Walt said he was getting ready to revamp "Tomorrowland" at Disneyland and had no time to think about a second park.

In a grand practical joke, a "source" told a local television station that the Ford Motor Company was purchasing the land. After the broadcast, the prankster sent a telegram to the station saying the land was to raise hay to feed the company's new Mustangs.

The *Sentinel* followed the land transactions, forty-seven in all covering 27,258 acres at a cost of $5,018,779. The newspaper joined in the speculation game, but it was no closer to finding out the real buyer. Everyone in town knew something was going to happen, but Disney kept its secret.

The *Sentinel* did break the story, but not in a way anyone could have anticipated. Journalists often receive invitations to visit a restaurant for a free meal, stay at a hotel for free, fly somewhere for free, all in the hope that the restaurant, hotel or resort will receive favorable publicity—and more business. They are called junkets.

Like many companies, Disney held junkets for journalists to show off new television shows or movies or give tours of Disneyland. In the fall of 1965, Disney issued invitations to a number of Florida reporters to visit Los Angeles. One invitation went to the *Sentinel* and ended up on the desk of Emily Bavar, the editor of the newspaper's Sunday magazine. She flew to California with five other reporters for an audience with Walt.

To Walt's surprise, Bavar asked him, "Mr. Disney, are you buying all that land in Orlando?" He offered stammering denials, but in his denials, Bavar found her story. Walt seemed to know far too much about the area—who else in California would know the average rainfall in Orlando? On October 16, 1965, she sent in her story speculating that the buyer was Disney. In Orlando, the newspaper treated the Bavar story as just more speculation in a long line of such stories. It appeared on page twenty-three.

Back in Orlando, Bavar met with Andersen and made the case for Disney. The following day, Andersen went further but was not quite ready to go all out: "Girl Reporter Convinced by Walt Disney."

On Sunday, Andersen was ready. Orlando residents—and the Disney executives who were in town—awoke to a large headline blaring: "We Say It's Disney"

Disney had kept the secret for eighteen months. There was one small problem: three hundred acres had not been purchased, and the price soared from an average of $200 to $1,000 an acre. Disney got everything it wanted except thirty acres.

The following day, Disney officials confirmed the *Sentinel*'s story. In mid-November, Walt and Roy Disney came to Orlando with Governor Haydon Burns to make the announcement at the Cherry Plaza Hotel on Lake Eola in downtown. It was Walt's only public appearance in Orlando. He was vague about what he was building, primarily because no one was quite sure what he was going to build. He said it would be about three years before it opened and cost $100 million just to "get the show on the road."

The announcement sent land prices soaring. A tract of 1,500 acres near Disney sold in 1964 for $168,000 and two years later sold for $2 million. What Walt seemed to have in mind was a park with two cities, the City of Yesterday and the City of Tomorrow. He did not want to build another amusement park—another Disneyland—but rather imagined a real city with real people living there. Walt read a number of books on urban planning and thought Disney World could be a utopian city, perhaps where employees of his theme park might live.

He called his vision the Experimental Prototype Community of Tomorrow—or EPCOT. It would have businesses, homes, schools, people movers, underground tunnels for moving garbage and even an airport.

In late 1966, Dial flew to California to see how Disneyland had affected Anaheim and to have lunch with Walt and Roy. Dial asked Walt a blunt question: "What would happen to this project if you walked out and got hit by a truck?" Walt said the project would continue under his brother, Roy.

Dial knew that Walt had been struggling with health problems but not that he was dying. Disney had lung cancer, although the company insisted he had been hospitalized to treat an old polo injury.

On December 15, 1966, Walt died. Within hours, Dial received a telephone call from a top Disney official asking if he remembered the conversation with Walt. He wanted Dial to reassure people in Orlando that the project would continue. Walt's death touched off rumors that the project was going to be canceled. One week later, Roy Disney made it clear that the project would continue.

But the question once again became what to build? Roy kept Walt's idea of a living city alive but made it clear that the amusement park would be built first. First, the company wanted to be granted certain governmental powers that would keep politicians in Orlando, Orange County or Osceola County from interfering with what Disney wanted to do. In 1967, Governor Claude Kirk signed a law that created three entities: Lake Buena Vista, Bay Lake and Reedy Creek Improvement District. The legislation is complicated, but basically, the Reedy Creek Improvement District operates much as a city, collecting property taxes from Disney and running city services.

Construction began on Walt Disney World—the new name in memory of Walt—in the fall of 1967. The original plan was to open in 1970, but demanding quality controls delayed it one year. Disney encountered a long list of problems, ranging from questions over which union had jurisdiction over things like monorails to problems with drainage of difficult terrain.

More than four thousand workers built Disney World, and they needed places to stay, touching off a building boom. Thousands more became park employees.

On October 1, 1971, Roy Disney opened the park. Within two years, Disney had twenty million visitors and gross sales of $3.2 billion and employed thirteen thousand people.

Roy Disney continued to insist that a city would be built, even as it abandoned the plans for a real city with residents. But Walt's city where "20,000 people would live and work and play" turned into a permanent world's fair with no residents.

In 1982, EPCOT opened, nothing like Walt had originally envisioned. In 1989, Disney-MGM Studios opened, followed by Animal Kingdom in 1998. Smaller attractions, such as Blizzard Beach and Typhoon Lagoon, also opened.

Originally, a family might come to Florida for a one-week vacation, spend a day or two at the Magic Kingdom and then go to the beach or another attraction. As Disney added attractions, more and more of the visitors' time was spent on Disney property. Disney added bus service from the airport and bus service connecting its parks, and tourists could spend their entire time in Florida without leaving Disney property.

Chapter 21

ATTRACTING OTHER ATTRACTIONS

N o sooner had Walt Disney announced his plans for a new park than others began making their own plans. Some were more dreams or schemes than real plans, and only a handful of the many on the drawing board ever became reality.

The first was George Millay, who originally planned to open an underwater restaurant in California. They idea did not work, but Millay came up with a theme park based on the sea, and SeaWorld San Diego was the result. Millay was an admirer of Walt Disney and wanted to imitate the qualities of Disneyland.

Millay opened SeaWorld Orlando in 1973. Millay also opened Wet 'n Wild, a water theme park. His two parks served as bookends on International Drive, a major tourist center.

Harcourt Brace Jovanovich, a book publisher, wanted to diversify into theme parks and purchased the company. The new owners encountered problems and sold out to Anheuser-Busch, creators of Busch Gardens. As part of the deal, Anheuser-Busch also had to buy two parks it did not want, Cypress Gardens in Winter Haven and Boardwalk and Baseball in Haines City.

SeaWorld later added Discovery Cove, where guests interact with dolphins and other marine animals. The small, exclusive park became a huge success. Admission is limited to keep the experience intimate.

Universal Studios traces its roots as a theme park back to 1905. Its founder, Carl Laemmle, charged visitors a nickel to watch movie production, and he provided a chicken lunch. The tour ended around 1930 with the rise of talking pictures—the tourists made too much noise. The tours came back in 1964.

From the time Disney announced plans for an Orlando park, there was speculation that Universal would follow suit. Universal, which underwent a number of ownership changes, had difficulty getting the park off the ground. It was not until 1990 that Universal Studios Florida opened. The park was a success, and Universal officials began planning for a second park, Islands of Adventure, which opened in 1999.

Universal also opened a shopping/dining/entertainment complex called CityWalk. Like Disney, Universal came to realize the value of hotels. Guests who stay at hotels on Disney property are much less likely to leave Disney, spending all of their vacation—and their money—at Disney attractions and restaurants. Universal originally opened the Portofino Bay Hotel—owned by Loews—and later two other Loews Hotels. Universal has announced plans to add more hotels and attractions. In 2010, Universal added the Wizarding World of Harry Potter, which drew enormous crowds.

Orlando's theme parks are among the most successful in the world, but for every success, there have been a dozen failures. One of the first to be proposed in the 1970s was Bible World, which did not go far beyond the announcement stage.

About the same time, promoters announced plans for Hurricane World— it was to be both a tourist attraction featuring simulated storms and a research center. Despite lots of promotion, it never got off the ground.

In 2005, the Paidia Company announced "Paidia's DestiNations Theme Park and Resort." It was supposed to open in 2007, but nothing happened.

When Universal Studios and Disney-MGM Studios opened, people began predicting that Orlando was about to become "Hollywood East." There was speculation that the city would be a lower-cost alternative to Hollywood for movies and television shows. There were some movies, such as *Parenthood*, filmed in Orlando, and a few television shows were made. Nickelodeon produced many of its early television shows here, but the biggest increase was in filming infomercials. Along with the dreams of Hollywood East came speculation that Paramount Studios, which operated theme parks, would build a studio and theme park in Orlando. The speculation continued for years, but Paramount showed no interest in Orlando and eventually sold off its theme parks.

One of the most promising proposals came from the King of the Cowboys, Roy Rogers. Rogers and his wife, Dale, held a press conference with Governor Haydon Burns to announce the development of a western theme park and dude ranch. Nothing came of the plan.

In 1990, magician Doug Henning announced plans to build Veda Land, a park combining magic and transcendental meditation. Before anything could happen, he announced that the project would move to Canada, near Niagara Falls. Henning died in 2000, but his project was already dead.

WinterWonderlando—the idea was to create winter in Orlando—never got beyond the announcement stage.

While some have been little more than pipe dreams, others have seemed possible and a few even seemed on their way. Orlando Thrill Park had everything: money, a great location, and experienced management. But it could not obtain the necessary permits. Neighbors protested, and the plan died—at least temporarily.

Some parks have started, and some have opened, only to meet with failure. One of the first to try and capitalize on the arrival of Disney was Circus World, originally owned by Ringling Bros. and Barnum & Bailey Circus. The idea was to make the park—nearly thirty miles from Orlando—the winter headquarters of the circus and turn it into an amusement park. A large building designed to look like a circus tent was built in 1974, and rides were added. There were daily circus performances, and a Wild West show was added. At the time, the circus was owned by Mattell, the toy company. In 1982, Mattel sold the circus but kept the park. Mattell added shows and rides, but it never became profitable. Harcourt Brace Jovanovich, which had purchased SeaWorld, also bought Cypress Gardens and Circus World.

Harcourt closed the park and switched to a new theme, naming it Boardwalk and Baseball and reopening in 1987. It was no more successful and closed in 1990.

For decades, there was speculation that Six Flags might open an amusement park in Orlando, despite dozens of denials. But Six Flags did come to Orlando once and met with disaster. In 1970, Six Flags bought a wax museum in California and decided to expand the concept to Orlando. In 1975, Six Flags Stars Hall of Fame Wax Museum opened next to Sea World and not far from Walt Disney World.

It had more than two hundred figures, some able to move. Attendance was good when it first opened, but as more competing attractions opened, fewer people went to Stars. Six Flags went looking for a buyer and found Harcourt Brace Jovanovich. But Harcourt was not interested in the wax museum; it merely wanted the building and the land and closed Stars. Harcourt Brace Jovanovich ran into its own economic problems in the late 1980s and sold off its theme park holdings.

Lewis Cartier made his fortune in British grocery stores, and when he sold out, he took a vacation to Orlando in 1972. While visiting Disney World, he came up with an idea for his own park—Little England. He moved quickly, purchasing land and assembling a team of veteran park operators. He obtained the permits, and construction began.

The 294-acre park was to be the centerpiece of the 1,350-acre resort, with residential housing, a golf course, a commercial area and a British village. Cartier saw it as a park that would attract American tourists and some of the tens of thousands of British tourists who might want a taste of home.

The attraction was scheduled to open in 1982, but the nation was in the midst of financial turmoil, and financial backers began to withdraw their pledges. Cartier sold off chunks of his land to keep going, but the few buildings he constructed were neglected and began to fall apart. Cartier's Little England never opened.

Splendid China seemed to have tremendous potential. Josephine Chen, a teacher and real estate developer, went to China in 1988 and met with officials of China Travel Services, a government agency. They took her to see a Splendid China park in Shenzhen. It featured miniatures of Chinese landmarks, including the Great Wall. It had been a tremendous success, drawing more than three million visitors its first year and repaying the initial investment of China Travel Services.

Chen and the Chinese government reached an agreement, and construction began near Orlando. Politics played a role as the park was built. The park would feature Buddhist shrines, including a Potala Palace, the home of the Dalai Lama, who was driven out of Tibet by the Chinese government.

As the park was about to open, China bought out Chen and took full control. It opened at the end of 1993, but almost immediately there were protests, including some by Buddhist monks. Some of the performers brought from China sought political asylum in the United States, and much of the media attention dealt with the problems at the park.

The problems discouraged people from attending. There was a major management shakeup, but the losses continued. At the end of 2003, the park closed.

The attractions of the parks brought more residents to the area. There were 51,826 in 1950, 88,135 in 1960 and 99,006 in 1970. Orange County grew from 114,950 in 1950 to 263,540 in 1960 and 344,311 in 1970.

Preserving History

The 1927 Orange County Courthouse building faced an uncertain fate until it became the Orange County Regional History Center. *Collection of author.*

IT WAS A LONG JOURNEY FROM A SMALL, *volunteer-run history museum with a hodgepodge collection to a nationally recognized professional museum. The dream began in the 1940s when Judge Donald A. Cheney sought to create a museum to preserve the records of Orange County, but it would be nearly sixty years before his dream became a reality. Cheney was the first director of the Orange County Historical Commission. Working with the Antiquarian Society, the county commission was asked to make it happen.*

In 1942, the first display opened in the 1892 courthouse—a collection of antiques and a pioneer kitchen. The museum had limited hours and was staffed by volunteers. It depended on donations and was more of an antique display than a true museum. The museum was only open three hours a week and drew an average of thirty people each week. It closed in the spring and summer.

After a dozen years, there was pressure to build a new building for the museum, but again the emphasis was on artifacts. The 1892 courthouse was in sorry shape and was condemned. Volunteers packed up the museum's holdings, and they went into storage for five years.

A new museum opened in 1963 on a floor of the new courthouse annex but again with very limited hours. In 1964, the county came up with $1,200 for a part-time secretary to catalog and file books and records, a small but significant step.

The museum moved again, to a space Cheney found to be unsatisfactory. In 1971, the Orange County Historical Society started a campaign to raise money for a new building.

The 1892 courthouse on the right was built when there was still plenty of empty land in downtown. Lake Eola is in the background. *Florida Photographic Collection.*

The new building in Loch Haven Park shared space with the science center. It had a number of displays but still was far short of being a true museum.

The museum might have carried on that way had it not been for three people: Sara Van Arsdel, Linda Chapin and Bill Donegan. Chapin was the chair of the Orange County Commission, Donegan was a commission member and Van Arsdel had taken over running the history museum in 1986.

At the time, the county was building a new courthouse, which meant that the old courthouse would be abandoned. There were two courthouse buildings, a beautiful five-story 1927 beaux arts building and an ugly 1960s modern addition with turquoise panels that was the rage in architecture at the time. Van Arsdel wanted the county to tear down the addition and turn the old courthouse over to her museum.

The courthouse sat at the spot where Orlando was founded, and there were plenty of suggestions about what the land, or the building could be used for. Chapin and Donegan— although from different political parties—banded together to preserve the courthouse. Donegan headed a task force designed to decide the fate of the building, and he steered the committee toward preservation. Donegan recommended saving the courthouse and using it as a museum.

The old courthouse was in far worse condition than people initially realized, and the cost of conversion rose dramatically, eventually reaching $35 million. Still, Chapin and Donegan remained faithful in their support, holding off critics who thought they were making a big mistake.

On September 29, 2000, the museum opened and since then has become a gathering place for the community.

The theme park Splendid China had strong financial backing but encountered a series of problems before closing. *Splendid China media kit.*

State Road 436 and Interstate 4 helped open up neighboring Seminole County as a major suburb. Near the Clay Springs community—a resort developed by Steinmetz—Everett Huskey developed Sweetwater Oaks for the upper middle class and the wealthy. Downtown, construction began on the nineteen-story CNA Tower, named for the Connecticut National Assurance Company. A sprawling office park went up about two miles from downtown.

The Disney success caught everyone by surprise. Visitors ended up staying at hotels fifty miles away. Developers responded with a hotel building boom that added tens of thousands of rooms. Unfortunately, everyone had the same idea at once, and what was a chronic shortage turned into a glut. When oil prices soared, gas lines wrapped around the block, and the number of tourists coming to Orlando dropped, the boom turned into a bust in 1974. Housing prices collapsed, and motels barely a year old declared bankruptcy. Dozens of projects stopped in the middle of construction. Shells of uncompleted buildings could be seen for years.

Chapter 22

THE NAVY LANDS AND
THE CITY GROWS

Disney was not the only newcomer bringing jobs. In 1968, the navy moved basic training activities from Bainbridge, Maryland, to Orlando. Politics played a role in the move. Martin Andersen, a friend of President Lyndon Johnson, lobbied hard for the base. Andersen had known Johnson since the 1940s and had endorsed him for president in 1960 when Johnson was running unsuccessfully for the nomination against John F. Kennedy.

The Orlando Naval Training Center came with six thousand employees and thousands of recruits—their numbers swollen by the Vietnam War. It became home of the Recruit Training Command and the Service School Command. In 1973, it became the only training facility for female recruits, and the nuclear power school also moved to Orlando. A full-service hospital replaced a smaller one in 1981 and became a Veterans Administration Outpatient Clinic. The facility closed in 1998, and the area became an upscale development known as Baldwin Park.

The University of Central Florida proved to be a major draw for many companies. Westinghouse opened a large facility next to UCF, which became part of the Siemens empire.

The population mix of Orlando began to change. The Cuban Revolution and communism under Fidel Castro sent thousands of Cubans fleeing to the United States, most to Miami. Over the decades, some of the Cubans moved to Orlando, but by 2010, they made up less than 2 percent of the population. In 1970, the number of Hispanics in Orange County schools was too small to measure. Thirty years later,

Martin Andersen, right, publisher of the *Sentinel*, with President Lyndon Johnson in 1964. Andersen and Johnson were friends, and the friendship helped land the navy training center in Orlando. *Orlando Sentinel.*

one out of five students was Hispanic. The growth was the result of the arrival of thousands of Puerto Ricans.

By 2010, there were nearly 300,000 Puerto Ricans in the Orlando area, the largest concentration outside of Puerto Rico and New York City. They are dubbed "Mickey Ricans," and Orlando's Azalea Park neighborhood is nicknamed "Little San Juan" because its population is half Puerto Rican.

The trend began in the 1970s when Landstar Homes, a leading home builder, began marketing homes to Puerto Ricans. The company placed advertisements in Puerto Rican newspapers urging Puerto Ricans to move to Orlando.

The campaign worked and other home builders followed Landstar's example. Landstar even opened an office in San Juan to sell Orlando homes directly.

At first, the advertisements drew Puerto Rican retirees looking for less crime and a reasonable cost of living. But gradually the builders began appealing to a wide range of Puerto Ricans. The appeal was obvious: a growing economy with thousands of theme park jobs opening up, a stable political climate and a crime rate that was half the rate in Puerto Rico.

The growth of the suburbs came at the expense of downtown shopping, and the growth of tourism around Walt Disney World meant the end for downtown hotels. The Downtowner Motel on Orange Avenue near city hall was torn down to make way for an office building. The Angebilt, once the finest in Central Florida, fell on hard times. By the 1970s, it attracted a seedier clientele and closed. The building avoided demolition when it became an office building. The San Juan, the city's first grand hotel, opened in the 1880s, but like the Angebilt, it could not compete with the new hotels outside of town. It was torn down and an office building erected.

Chapter 23

MAGIC FOR ORLANDO

For years, Orlando had flirted with professional sports teams, always hoping to land one but falling short. In the late 1980s, Pat Williams, a former executive of the Philadelphia 76ers, came to town and became a pied piper, trying to convince Orlando that it could land a National Basketball Association team. Many dismissed him out of hand, but some believed that his dream could be real. He convinced respected businessmen James and Robert Hewitt, and they attracted other investors.

Still it seemed like a long shot. The competition was tough, and originally the league was going to add three teams with one going to Florida. That meant that either Miami or Orlando would get a team, with Charlotte and Minnesota getting franchises.

The NBA agreed to give both Miami and Orlando teams, but with a condition for Orlando. The Hewitts and their partners had enough financial strength to buy the franchise, but the NBA wanted a single lead partner and found William DuPont III, who seemed to have the financial resources to carry the team.

The team held a contest to choose a name and more than four thousand entries poured in. The four finalists were Heat, Tropics, Juice and Magic. Magic won.

The expansion fee was reportedly $32.5 million, and Matt Guokas became the first head coach. In June 1989, the team chose Nick Anderson as its first draft pick.

The Magic played its first game at the new Orlando Arena against the New Jersey Nets, losing by five points. Two days later, they won their first game, against the New York Knicks.

Trials of Orlando

ORLANDO HAS BEEN THE SETTING FOR TWO TRIALS *that made national headlines. The first, in 1980, featured mass murderer Ted Bundy; the second was in 2011 when Casey Anthony went on trial for the murder of her young daughter, Caylee.*

Ted Bundy began his murderous spree in 1974 and, before being caught in 1978, killed thirty women in seven states. His killing spree brought him to Tallahassee on January 8, 1978. One week later, he broke into the Chi Omega sorority house and killed two women and seriously beat two others. On February 8, he was in Lake City, where he murdered twelve-year-old Kimberly Diane Leach and placed her remains in a state park. Four days later, he was captured in Pensacola driving a stolen car.

He went on trial in Miami for the sorority house murders in 1979 and tried to handle his own defense. It was a disaster, and Bundy was convicted and sentenced to death.

The trial for the murder of Kimberly Leach was moved to Orlando. It did not draw the interest that the first trial had but still attracted reporters from throughout the country. Bundy was already facing the death penalty, and this trial was anticlimactic and the evidence overwhelming. The jury deliberated eight hours before returning a verdict of guilty.

The most unusual thing about the trial came during the penalty phase, when he called Carole Ann Boone to the stand as a character witness. As she testified, Bundy proposed to her, and she accepted. Bundy declared in court that they were legally married. He and Boone were taking advantage of a little-known Florida law that a declaration of marriage before a judge in court made a marriage legal.

He was sentenced to death again. A lengthy appeals progress began. Even though he had been convicted of the sorority murders first, that appeals process dragged out, and Bundy ended up being executed on January 24, 1989, for the Leach murder.

The Orlando trial was held in the ornate 1927 courthouse, which later became the Orange County History Center. Someone—but not Bundy—carved his initials into the defense table, and the legend grew that it was Bundy. That would assume that court officials let him have a sharp instrument to do the carving. No one knows where the initials came from, but they became an attraction in the museum, and officials had to place a piece of clear plastic over them to keep away anyone who might damage the initials that Ted Bundy did not make.

The Bundy trial took place in a different era; television news was limited to the three networks and thirty minutes of news each night. Although the case was sensational, there was no live coverage from the courtroom, even though cameras were allowed. Stations showed excerpts on the evening news.

Everything had changed when Casey Anthony went on trial in 2011. Not only had twenty-four-hour news arrived, but there were cable stations dedicated to covering trials.

On July 15, 2008, Casey Anthony told her parents that her babysitter had taken her daughter Caylee and her mother called 911 to report her granddaughter missing. The following day, Casey was arrested for child neglect, making false statements and obstructing an investigation.

Almost immediately, the story captivated the nation, and the interest heightened on October 14 when she was indicted on first-degree murder charges. Prosecutors eventually decided to seek the death penalty. Casey hired little-known attorney Jose Baez.

Cable networks such as HLN saw their ratings spike as the case dragged on. On May 24, 2011, the trial opened in Orlando. Across the street from the towering courthouse was a huge empty lot where television stations and networks set up their trucks, turning a dusty block into an electronic city that broadcast twenty-four hours a day.

The jury came from St. Petersburg because of pretrial publicity in Orlando, although it is difficult to imagine anyone in the country who had not heard of the case. Each morning at dawn, lines formed as people hoped to get one of the few seats in the courtroom. The courthouse became a tourist attraction; people came to Orlando for Disney World, Universal Studios and the Casey Anthony trial. Cars with out-of-state license plates drove by slowly, snapping pictures of the courthouse on one side of the street and the television city on the other side.

The nation came to believe overwhelmingly that Casey Anthony was guilty, but on July 5, she was found not guilty of the murder charge. Even after the verdict, the nation's captivation with Casey continued. Whether it was speculation about where she was living, or his bankruptcy, she could still draw the attention of the nation.

On the court, the young team was mediocre—posting a 31–51 record—but at the box office, it was a hit, selling out forty of forty-one home games.

The team was a financial success, but off the court, DuPont encountered financial setbacks and, in 1991, sold the team to Rich DeVos, co-founder of the giant Amway Company and a man with more than a billion dollars behind him.

The Magic hit the jackpot on May 17, 1992, when they won the first pick in the NBA draft and chose Shaquille O'Neal, a seven-foot-one-inch center who changed the fortunes of the Magic.

The following year, the Magic again won the NBA lottery, even though they only had one chance, and chose Penny Hardaway and went on to win fifty games but lost in the first round of the playoffs. In 1994–95, the Magic obtained Horace Grant and won fifty-seven games. They advanced to the NBA finals but lost to the Houston Rockets in four games.

The Amway Center opened in 2010 as the home of the Orlando Magic. *Orlando Magic.*

O'Neal became the first in a string of big-name players to leave Orlando, decamping for the Los Angeles Lakers, the first of a number of stops. Penny Hardaway then became the team leader but not in the way fans had hoped. Hardaway was the leader of a player revolt against coach Brian Hill. Management fired Hill.

After Hardaway left, the team signed Grant Hill and Tracy McGrady. Hill left for Phoenix, McGrady became unhappy and left, and Doc Rivers was dismissed as coach.

Dwight Howard came to the Magic directly from high school in 2004 and had an immediate impact. Still there was more turmoil, coaching changes and disappointments.

As with O'Neal, Hardaway and McGrady, Howard became unhappy with the Magic. Once again the team fired the coach, and Howard left for the Los Angeles Lakers and then the Houston Rockets.

When talk of obtaining an NBA team began in the mid-1980s, Orlando seemed like a long shot. The city had no arena and quickly built one that was serviceable but lacked many of the amenities that became staples of other NBA arenas. Within a dozen years of the first tipoff, the Magic began campaigning for a new arena. An economic downturn delayed their initial

160

hopes, but in 2006, Mayor Buddy Dyer agreed to build a $480-million facility with the Magic contributing some money.

The Magic have been a rare success for the city that has seen sports teams come and go for half a century. Usually the team—and frequently the entire league—folded, leaving behind piles of unpaid bills and disappointed fans.

Still, the mere mention that another professional team—no matter how obscure the sport or unlikely success—sends the city into a frenzy, with leaders promising to roll out the red carpet.

The city's first professional sports team was the Orlando Panthers, a member of the Continental Football League. They came to Orlando in 1966 and were actually one of the town's most successful teams, lasting four years and featuring the first female player—placekick holder Patricia Palinkas. She held the ball for her husband, Steve, the kicker. The team and the league folded in 1970.

In 1974, the World Football League gave Orlando a franchise, the Blazers. Jack Pardee was the coach and recalled that he had to bring toilet paper from home for the locker room because the team could not afford to buy any. The team had started as the Baltimore-Washington Ambassadors, then just the Washington Ambassadors and finally the Virginia Ambassadors of Norfolk. Hoping that a WFL franchise might lead to a franchise in the National Football League, the Baltimore/Washington/Norfolk Ambassadors became the Florida Blazers. The team was a success on the field, but the league and the team were a disaster financially. During the season, there was talk of moving the team again, this time to Atlanta. "It's hard to concentrate on football when so many rumors of a franchise shift are making the rounds," Pardee said.

The team stopped paying players, and attendance suffered. A financial savior seemed to emerge, displaying a $1.5 million dollar check on television and promising a complicated $100 million deal. The check turned out to be from an account of an ex-convict and bounced. The Blazers folded, but that did not stop the city's interest in professional sports.

The Orlando Renegades were part of the United States Football League and played a single season in 1985. As with the Blazers, the team had started out in Washington but ended up in Orlando with Lee Corso as head coach. The original idea was that the league would play when the NFL was not playing. But Donald Trump purchased the New Jersey Generals and convinced the league to take on the NFL head to head. The entire league folded.

Orlando did get a National Football League team—sort of. The league created the World League of American Football in an effort to expand

Bay Hill

ARNOLD PALMER IS KNOWN AROUND THE WORLD *for his greatness as a golfer, but in Orlando he is also known as the man behind some of the great residential developments, including Bay Hill and Isleworth.*

To millions of Americans, Bay Hill is a golf course and home to Arnold Palmer's annual golf tournament. But it was one of the first suburban communities in Orlando.

Dr. Phillip Phillips was the largest landowner in Orange County, and in 1954, he sold off his citrus land but kept his uncultivated property, which he named Bay Hill. He had begun making plans in the 1940s for the development of Bay Hill. He developed his plan to every detail, making sure it did not damage the environment in an era when the word was almost unheard of. He wanted to preserve the lakes and to establish water-retention basins.

In the late 1950s, the Professional Golf Association was looking for a new place to build its headquarters. The group wanted to move from its location near Clearwater, and the son of Dr. Phillips, Howard Phillips, suggested Bay Hill. He offered a 640-acre tract, but the PGA decided to move to South Florida instead.

But the 640 acres did interest a group that wanted to build a golf course, and the Bay Hill Club was born. The golf group wanted a world-class golf course, but Howard Phillips was most interested in building a residential community that would serve as a model for preserving green space.

At first, it did not go as Howard Phillips dreamed; people were interested in the golf course but showed little interest in building homes. The coming of Disney World brought some residents, but it was still viewed as too remote. It was Arnold Palmer who made the club and the neighborhood. In 1976, Palmer bought Bay Hill and upgraded the course to meet PGA standards. Soon, homesites were selling briskly and what was an isolated community became an upscale suburb.

football around the world. It was a minor-league version of the NFL. The Thunder drew an average of nineteen thousand in its first season and sixteen thousand its second year. The team folded in 1992 while the league held on for several more years. The team did have one distinction: ESPN voted its jerseys the second-worst football jersey in history.

The Orlando Rollergators were the first of two roller hockey teams in the city. The Rollergators lasted a season and became the Orlando Jackals, which did not fare any better.

The Orlando Wahoos played two seasons in the Women's Pro Softball League, drawing a paltry three hundred to four hundred fans each game.

The World Wrestling Entertainment formed the XFL in 2001, and Orlando landed a franchise in 2001, the Rage. The eight-team league lasted just one season, a victim of terrible television ratings.

There was indoor soccer in 2007–08 from the Orlando Sharks, which folded, although the league continued to operate. The NBA's Women's National Basketball Association had an Orlando team from 1999 to 2002, the Miracle, but the team failed to draw, despite the deep pockets of its owners, the Orlando Magic. In 2003, the team moved to Connecticut and found success.

Several hockey teams have played in Orlando. The Orlando Solar Bears were backed by the Orlando Magic and found some success, but the league struggled and folded. The Orlando Seals played from 2002 to 2004 as part of two minor hockey leagues. A new team and league, but using the Solar Bears name, returned in 2012 and has attracted a following.

The newest team is the Orlando City Soccer club, which has drawn impressive numbers.

Chapter 24

THE THREE HURRICANES

For those who lived through it, 2004 will always be remembered as the year of the three hurricanes. Orlando had never seen anything like it. The storms came within six weeks, deluging a city unprepared for a storm. The last hurricane threat had been forty-four years earlier, and that was a tropical storm by the time it reached Orlando. No one living in Orlando had seen hurricane-force winds spread through Central Florida.

Hurricane Charley was the first, hitting Cuba and heading toward Florida with winds of 150 miles per hour. It came ashore on Captiva Island on the southwest coast on August 13 and headed inland. By the early morning hours of the August 14, it began to move across Orlando with winds gusting up to 106 miles per hour. It did not stay long, passing over Daytona Beach two hours later, but the damage was devastating.

Thousands of homes were without roofs, many were flooded and power was out nearly everywhere. The loss of electricity forced stores to close, and there was no food available. Across Orlando, huge blue tarps covered leaking or missing roofs, and some remained there for more than a year. For the first time, Walt Disney World closed because of a hurricane.

Orlando barely began to recover when Hurricane Frances began forming in the Atlantic. It eventually reached winds of 140 miles an hour and became a Category 4 storm. By the time it came ashore on September 5 near Stuart, it was a category 2 storm with 105-mile-per-hour winds. As it moved across the Florida Peninsula, it was not nearly as powerful as Hurricane Charley and went well South of Orlando. The problem was that it moved slowly and took about seven hours to cross the peninsula. Orlando's lakes could not stand any additional water, and there was more flooding and power outages. There was tremendous damage to citrus crops, and $100 million dollars to facilities at Cape Canaveral. Schools were closed, and businesses were forced to close their doors because of flooding or power shortages. Again, Walt Disney World closed.

Hurricane Ivan came through the Gulf of Mexico in mid-September but headed for the Louisiana coast. It brought some rain to Orlando, but an already jittery city stocked up on water and food and expected the worst.

The final storm was Hurricane Jeanne, which hit Florida in the same area as Frances, and followed a path well South of Orlando as it headed toward Tampa and the Gulf of Mexico. It brought another 5.4 inches of rain to Orlando, which was already drenched. The impact of Jeanne was to make a terrible situation worse. Trees that had survived the two earlier storms now gave way and again many people lost power.

Chapter 25

THE NEW MILLENNIUM

Orlando has always experienced a boom-and-bust economy. The rapid growth of the 1880s was followed by the freeze of the 1890s, the unprecedented growth of the 1920s was followed by the Florida land bust and then the Great Depression and the growth after the opening of Disney World stopped with the gasoline shortages in the mid-1970s.

The economy was doing well in 2001—there was talk of a massive civil improvement program, including a new arena and a light-rail system—when terrorists struck on September 11. Immediately, flights were canceled, and vacation plans were scrapped. Tourism declined in 2001 and then began a steady climb upward.

When the economy began to falter in 2005, tourism declined again. Not only did tourism decline, but the housing bubble also hit Orlando particularly hard. The city consistently places on the list of cities with the most home foreclosures, and home building came to a virtual stop and unemployment rose.

The housing market peaked in 2005, with thirty-seven thousand homes sold in the Orlando area. In 2006, it fell by 11 percent, an unbelievable 40 percent drop came in 2007 and another 10 percent in 2008. From the high of thirty-seven thousand homes sold in 2005, the market dropped to eighteen thousand in 2008. The market began to come back in 2009, but many of the sales were foreclosed homes dumped on the market at low prices. It wasn't until 2013 that the region came close to matching the 2005 sales.

Despite the economic downturn, the city embarked on an ambitious building program. Backed by taxes on tourists, the city built a new arena and a new performing arts center, renovated the city's football stadium and made plans to build a soccer stadium.

From a collection of log cabins in 1850 and a handful of residents, Orlando became the twenty-seventh-largest metropolitan area in the nation by 2013 and the third largest in Florida. Up until World War II, most Americans had never heard of Orlando, but by 2013, a survey showed that when asked where they wanted to live, Orlando finished fourth among those polled.

Once, there had been orange groves along Orange Avenue south of downtown. Gradually, stores, offices and homes replaced them. By 1977, there was only one grove still standing, owned by Mary Compton and taking up an entire block. She was one of the state's leading horticulturalists, and her property was famous for its beautiful gardens. In 1976, Compton died at the age of ninety-three, and her fifty-year-old home and her orange trees were torn down to make way for a shopping center. After one hundred years, there were no longer any orange groves on Orange Avenue.

Appendix I

ORLANDO MAYORS

ONE-YEAR TERMS

William J. Brack	1875–76
J.H. Allen	1877
Charles H. Munger	1878
A.M. Hyer	1879
R.L. Summerlin	1880
C.D. Sweet	1881
C.A. Boone	1882
J.L. Bryan	1883–84
E.J. Reel	1885–86
F.S. Chapman	1887
Mathew R. Marks	1888–90
W.L. Palmer	1891–93
Mahlon Gore	1894–96
J.B. Parramore	1896–1902
B.M. Robinson	1903–04
J.H. Smith	1905–06

Orlando Mayor Buddy Dyer. *City of Orlando.*

Braxton Beacham	1907
William H. Jewell	1908–10
W.H. Reynolds	1911–13

THREE-YEAR TERMS

E.F. Sperry	1914–16*
James L. Giles	1916–19
E.G. Duckworth	1920–24
James L. Giles	1924–25
Samuel Y. Way	1932–34
V.W. Estes	1935–37
Samuel Y. Way	1938–40
William Beardall	1941–52
J. Rolfe Davis	1953–56

FOUR-YEAR TERMS

Robert S. Carr	1956–67*
Carl T. Langford	1967–80
Bill Frederick	1980–92
Glenda Hood	1992–2003
Buddy Dyer	2003–

*Died in office

ORANGE COUNTY CHAIRMEN/MAYORS

David Mizell	1860–71
James G. Speer	1872–73
William H. Holden	1874–75
John R. Mizell	1876
James G. Speer	1877
James M. Owens	1878–80
King Wylley	1881–85
Clinton Johnson	1885–86
B.F. Whitner	1887–89
C.E. Smith	1890–92
A.C. Martin	1893
J.A. McDowell	1894
J.N. Whitner	1895–96
H.H. Dickson	1897–1907
J.H. Lee	1908–10
M.O. Overstreet	1911–19
Arthur Schultz	1920–24

Orange County mayor Teresa Jacobs. *Orange County government.*

L.L. Payne	1925–29
S.S. Sadler	1930
V.W. Estes	1931–32
S.J. Sligh	1933–34
Carl Jackson	1935
Henry A. Porter	1936
Carl Jackson	1937–40
J. Rolfe Davis	1941–42
E.D. Cook	1943–44
V.E. Borland	1945
Maynard H. Evans	1946
V.E. Borland	1947
W.W. Pharr	1948
Maynard H. Evans	1949

Harry P. Witherington	1950
S.P.H. Harrison	1951
A.D. Mims	1952
John H. Talton	1953
John T. Murdock Jr.	1954
James T. Cooper	1955
Jack W. McDowell	1956
A.D. Mims	1957
John T. Murdock Jr.	1958
James T. Cooper	1959
Jack W. McDowell	1960
A.D. Mims	1960
F.B. Surguine Jr.	1961
John H. Talton	1962
Donald S. Evans	1963–64
John H. Talton	1965
S.B. Surguine Jr.	1966
James T. Cooper	1967–68
Paul Pickett	1968–70
Ralph Poe	1971
Paul Pickett	1972–73
Jack Martin	1974
Ben Benham	1975

ELECTED MAYORS

Linda Chapin	1990–98
Mel Martinez	1998–2001
Richard Crotty	2001–11
Teresa Jacobs	2011–

POPULATION GROWTH

Year	Orlando	Orange County
1850	—	466
1860	—	987
1870	—	2,195
1880	200	6,618
1890	2,856	12,584
1900	2,481	11,374
1910	3,894	19,107
1920	9,282	19,890
1930	27,330	49,737
1940	36,736	70,074
1950	51,826	114,074
1960	88,135	263,540
1970	99,006	344,311
1980	128,251	471,016
1990	164,693	677,491
2000	185,951	896,344
2010	238,300	1,145,956

BIBLIOGRAPHY

Argrett, LeRoy. *A History of the Black Community of Orlando, Florida*. Fort Bragg, CA: Cypress House Press, 1991.

Bacon, Eve. *Orlando: A Centennial History*. Chuluota, FL: Mickler House, 1975–77.

Beatty, Robert L., II. "Legacy to the People: Community and the Orange County Regional History Center." MA thesis, University of Central Florida, 2002.

Boyd, Valerie. *Wrapped in Rainbows: the Life of Zora Neale Hurston*. New York: Scribner, 2003.

Brotemarkle, Benjamin D. *Beyond the Theme Parks: Exploring Central Florida*. Gainesville: University Press of Florida, 1999.

Cardona, Cynthia. "The Emergence of Central Florida's Puerto Rican Community." MA thesis, University of Central Florida, 2007.

Clark, James C. *Presidents in Florida: How the Presidents Have Shaped Florida and How Florida Has Influenced the Presidents*. Sarasota, FL: Pineapple Press, 2012.

———. *200 Quick Looks at Florida History*. Sarasota, FL: Pineapple Press, 2000.

Covington, James W. *The Seminoles of Florida*. Gainesville: University Press of Florida, 1993.

Dickinson, Joy. *Remembering Orlando: Tales from Elvis to Disney*. Charleston, SC: The History Press, 2006.

Dickinson, Joy Wallace. *Orlando: City of Dreams*. Charleston, SC: Arcadia, 2003.

Duany, Jorge. "Mickey Ricans? The Recent Puerto Rican Diaspora to Florida." Paper presented at the conference of the Institute for the Study of Latin America and the Caribbean, University of South Florida, Tampa, October 13–20, 2012.

Edwards, Wynette. *Orlando and Orange County*. Charleston, SC: Arcadia, 2001.

Foglesong, Richard E. *Married to the Mouse: Walt Disney World and Orlando*. New Haven, CT: Yale University Press, 2001.

Fries, Kena. *Orlando in the Long, Long Ago...and Now*. Orlando, FL: Florida Press, Inc., 1938.

Gabler, Neal. *Walt Disney: The Triumph of the American Imagination*. New York: Knopf, 2006.

Gannon, Michael. *The New History of Florida*. Gainesville, FL: University Press of Florida, 1996.

Gore, E.H. *From Florida Sand to "The City Beautiful," A Historical Record of Orlando, Florida*. Winter Park, FL: Orange Press, 1951.

Hanna, Alfred Jackson, and Kathryn Abbey Hanna. *Florida's Golden Sands*. Indianapolis: Bobbs-Merrill, 1950.

Holic, Nathan. *University of Central Florida*. Charleston, SC: Arcadia, 2009.

Homan, Lynn M., and Thomas Reilly. *Orlando in Vintage Postcards*. Charleston, SC: Arcadia, 2001.

Kealing, Bob. *Kerouac in Florida: Where the Road Ends*. Orlando: Arbiter Press, 2004.

———. *Tupperware, Unsealed: Brownie Wise, Earl Tupper, and the Home Party Pioneers*. Gainesville: University Press of Florida, 2008.

Kendrick, Baynard. *Orlando: A Century Plus*. Orlando, FL: Sentinel Star Co., 1976.

Porter, Tana Mosley. *Historic Orange County: The Story of Orlando and Orange County*. Orlando, FL: Historical Pub. Network, 2009.

Powers, Ormund. *Fifty Years: The Sun Bank Story, 1934–1984*. Orlando, FL: Sun Bank, N.A., 1984.

———. *Martin Andersen: Editor, Publisher, Galley Boy*. Chicago: Contemporary Books, 1996.

Rajtar, Steve. *A Guide to Historic Orlando*. Charleston, SC: The History Press, 2006.

Rajtar, Steve, and Gayle Prince Rajtar. *A Guide to Historic Winter Park, Florida*. Charleston, SC: The History Press, 2008.

Robison, Jim, and Mark Andrews. *Flashbacks: the Story of Central Florida's Past*. Orlando, FL: Orange County Historical Society and the Orlando Sentinel, 1995.

Shofner, Jerrell H. *History of Apopka and Northwest Orange County, Florida.* Tallahassee, FL: Sentry Press, 1982.

————. *Orlando: The City Beautiful.* Tulsa, OK: Continental Heritage Press, 1984.

Spencer, Donald D. *Greetings from Orlando & Winter Park.* Atglen, PA: Schiffer Pub., 2008.

Swanson, Henry F. *Countdown for Agriculture in Orange County, Florida.* Orlando: Henry F. Swanson, 1975.

Thompson, Geraldine Fortenberry. *Orlando Florida.* Charleston, SC: Arcadia, 2003.

INDEX

Y

ABOUT THE AUTHOR

James C. Clark is a member of the history faculty at the University of Central Florida, where he has taught since 1987. He has become one of the leading Florida historians and the author of eight books. He has been a resident of Orlando since 1975. He received his doctorate in Florida history from the University of Florida.

Visit us at
www.historypress.net

·······································

This title is also available as an e-book